Rob Green studied theology at King's College, London, and trained for ordained ministry in the Church of England at Wycliffe Hall, Oxford. He spent over thirty years in parish ministry mostly on the staff of Norbury Parish Church, Hazel Grove. For nine of those years he also trained Readers (lay ministers) in the Diocese of Chester. He retired in 2019 but continues to write and blogs at revrobgreen.wordpress.com.

To my wonderful family, to the people of Norbury Parish Church, Hazel Grove, and to Keith and Avril, without whom this book would not have seen the light of day.

Robert Green

ON THE BIBLE'S BACK ROADS

Where Old Stories and Our
Stories Meet

AUSTIN MACAULEY PUBLISHERS™
LONDON * CAMBRIDGE * NEW YORK * SHARJAH

Copyright © Robert Green 2024

The right of Robert Green to be identified as author of this work has been asserted by the author in accordance with sections 77 and 78 of the Copyright, Designs and Patents Act 1988.

All rights reserved. No part of this publication may be reproduced, stored in a retrieval system, or transmitted in any form or by any means, electronic, mechanical, photocopying, recording, or otherwise, without the prior permission of the publishers.

Any person who commits any unauthorised act in relation to this publication may be liable to criminal prosecution and civil claims for damages.

The story, experiences, and words are the author's alone.

A CIP catalogue record for this title is available from the British Library.

ISBN 9781398455894 (Paperback)
ISBN 9781398455917 (ePub e-book)
ISBN 9781398455900 (Audiobook)

www.austinmacauley.co.uk

First Published 2024
Austin Macauley Publishers Ltd®
1 Canada Square
Canary Wharf
London
E14 5AA

I would like to offer grateful thanks to the following who have greatly assisted with the writing of this book. My wife Hilary encouraged me throughout the writing process. Keith and Avril Ravenscroft also gave much support and encouragement. Keith read the manuscript in stages as it was written and provided invaluable feedback – it kept me going! Keith, I can't thank you enough. Susan Jones read the manuscript and made some thoughtful and helpful suggestions. Keith and Avril Ravenscroft, Richard Lawry, Ann Whitehead and more recently Val Hindmarsh, Patrick Angier and Sue Hawkins have all encouraged me to consider exploring the possibility of being published. Members of a number of local church congregations road tested this book and responded so positively to it. Lastly but not least the team at Austen Macauley Publishers worked hard to get this book to the finish line.

Table of Contents

Introduction	13
Cain: 'Am I my brother's keeper' (Ash Wednesday)	15
Lot: 'Flee for your lives'	18
Hagar and Ishmael: 'God heard the boy crying'	21
Melchizedek: 'You are a priest for ever'	24
Jochebed: 'When she could hide him no longer'	27
Bezalel and Oholiab: 'See I have chosen'	30
Jethro: 'The work is too heavy for you'	33
Balaam: 'I could not…go beyond the command of the Lord'	36
Rahab: 'She tied the scarlet cord'	39
Deborah: 'I, Deborah, arose'	42
Jephthah and his daughter: 'She was an only child'	45
Ruth: 'Your people will be my people'	48
Jonathan: 'You were very dear to me'	52
Mephibosheth: 'For I will surely show you only kindness'	55
Bathsheba and Uriah: 'You are the man!'	58
Omri: 'But Omri did evil'	61
The Widow at Zarephath: 'The jar of flour will not be used up'	64
Hananiah, Mishael and Azariah: 'Look, I see four men'	67
Esther: 'If it pleases the king'	71

Haggai: 'Because of my house, which remains a ruin'	75
Joseph: 'Joseph her husband was a righteous man'	79
Simeon: 'My eyes have seen your salvation'	83
The Samaritan Woman: 'I who speak to you am he'	86
The Paralytic: 'Take your mat and go home'	90
The Woman Subject to Bleeding: 'Your faith has healed you'	94
The One Who Is 'For Us': 'He was not one of us'	98
The Widow of Nain: 'I say to you, get up'	102
Mary and Martha: 'Mary has chosen what is better'	105
The Man Healed of Leprosy: 'Were not all ten cleansed'	108
Zacchaeus: 'Today salvation has come to this house'	111
The Woman Caught in Adultery: 'Go now and leave your life of sin'	114
The Centurion: 'Go! It will be done just as you believed it would'	117
The Canaanite Woman: 'Woman, you have great faith!' (Passion Sunday)	121
The Little Children: 'The kingdom of God belongs to such as these'	125
Stephen: 'And Saul was there, giving approval'	128
Tabitha: 'Tabitha, get up!'	132
Ananias: 'Brother Saul'	135
Lydia: 'The Lord opened her heart'	138
Bartimaeus: 'Jesus, Son of David, have mercy on me'	141
The Member of the Crowd: 'Hosanna to the Son of David!' (Palm Sunday)	144
The Widow at the Temple: 'She, out of her poverty, put in everything'	147
The Spies: 'They were unable to trap him'	151
The Woman with the Alabaster Jar: 'You will not always have me'	155

The Disciple Whom Jesus Loved: 'Lord, who is it?' (Maundy Thursday)   158

The Repentant Criminal: 'Today you will be with me
in paradise' (Good Friday)   162

Joseph of Arimathea: 'He asked for Jesus' body'   166

Cleopas and his Companion: 'Were not our hearts burning within us'
(Easter Day)   169

Introduction

In his semi-autobiographical novel David Copperfield, Charles Dickens brings to life a wonderful collection of minor characters we encounter as the novel progresses. They include the indefatigable Barkis, who never misses an opportunity to express his willingness to marry Clara Peggoty; the scheming and manipulative Uriah Heep, always ever so 'umble; Mr Micawber, who never quite gets his personal finances in order until he goes to Australia and Betsy Trotwood, perpetually worried by encroaching donkeys. They all play their part in the narrative of David Copperfield's life and his story wouldn't be the same without them.

As we read the Bible there are, of course, several major characters such as Abraham, Moses, Elijah, Peter, Paul and, above all, Jesus himself who shape the narrative and are fundamental to our understanding of what it all means. But there are also a host of minor characters, some of whom, like the strange and unknown priest Melchizedek who greets Abraham at Salem (the future Jerusalem) following his success in battle, who whilst only appearing briefly, (in his case in three verses, Genesis 14:18-20) enrich the story and open windows through which we can see more fully the nature and purposes of God. Significantly the writer to the Hebrews uses Melchizedek to offer us an insight into the nature of Christ's priesthood; something which occupies more verses than his original appearance to provide refreshments for Abraham.

In this series of reflections, we are going to consider a number of these minor characters, some of whom may be quite unfamiliar, and see what we can learn from them. They were not all paragons of virtue and, like us, were flawed human beings. But their stories are included in the biblical narrative for a reason; they have found a place in God's word to us because they help us to better understand the story of God's revelation to us in Jesus Christ.

This book is designed to be read at any time but you or your church may wish to study it specifically during Lent. There are 47 reflections, one for each day in Lent (including Sundays) and the principal holy days are shown in brackets in the title of the corresponding day's study. At the end of each reflection there are some questions you might like to consider. There may, of course, be other questions that come to mind that are worth exploring. There is also a short prayer but please feel free to make your own prayer response.

A note on referencing. When referencing from the passage for the day when it is contained within a single chapter the verse or verses only will be referenced, as in (v 6; v 3–5). If the reading contains verses from two chapters it will be chapter and verse, as in (6:7). All other references contain book, chapter, and verse(s) as in (Romans 8:17).

Cain: Genesis 4:1-17
'Am I my brother's keeper' (v 9)
(Ash Wednesday)

The Old Testament takes a keen interest in fraternal relationships (I grew up with three brothers so have a bit of background here!). Interestingly on several occasions it is younger brothers, sometimes deservedly (Joseph) and sometimes by deft use of skulduggery (Jacob) who gain the upper hand. In the story of Cain and Abel, God's apparent preference for the younger rather than the older brother's sacrifice leads to an envy fuelled act of fratricide. It is worth noting, before going any further, that we shouldn't get too hung up about how literally to take this story; going round in ever decreasing circles wondering who Cain's wife and the 'whoever' in verse 14 could have been if Adam and Eve were the first two human beings leads us nowhere. As we are about to see, the teller of this story is challenging us with some much more significant and relevant questions.

It isn't entirely clear why God favoured the offering of Abel. It could be argued that he had taken a bit more care in choosing some of the very best of his flock to offer but the text offers nothing definitive – God simply made his choice. It is, however, in the violent response of Cain that the warning this story embodies is to be found. He considers himself slighted; hardly surprising when, in the cultural setting from which this story arose, it was the firstborn son who should have had everything going for him. We see this reflected at their respective births; when Cain is born Eve expresses a delight entirely missing from the birth of her second son Abel (v 1-2). The continuing use in the context of royal succession of the adage 'the heir and the spare' contains a faint echo of this.

Cain's fury at having been apparently snubbed and his deadly jealousy that his younger brother had, in his eyes, put one over on him reflect a sense of entitlement that we recognise as being very much present in the world in which we live. It often manifests itself in a feeling of superiority leading to an over developed sense of one's own importance, unrealistic demands on other people and an overweening desire for power and influence. It follows that when these needs are unmet there is considerable potential for conflict. Such attitudes exist in government and in all parts of society and are not entirely unknown in church life.

It is Cain's sense of entitlement and resultant outrage that God has not recognised his intrinsic superiority as the elder brother, effectively cheating him of the recognition that he believed was his by right, that leads him to take the life of an entirely innocent younger sibling. And one terrible mistake then leads to another as he tries to lie his way out of it with his rhetorical and immortalised question, 'am I my brother's keeper?' (v 9 – roughly translated as 'search me, guv').

The point for us is that Cain's deep-seated rage, an anger that is a grown up and much more lethal form of throwing one's toys out of the pram, has got out of control, and mastered him entirely. Before continuing one thing needs to be made clear; anger isn't always destructive and self-centred. It can be an appropriate response to injustice. Attitudes and actions involving nations, communities and individuals that cause poverty, disempowerment, prejudice, despair, and death should make us angry enough to want to get out of our seats and do something about it. Jesus got into a furious rage with those who had desecrated the Temple by squeezing money from those already very badly off to line their own pockets (Matthew 21:12-13). He was quite unable to stand to one side and leave it unchallenged. It is surely very appropriate, in the face of global trading arrangements that benefit rich countries over poor ones, elections being rigged so that despots can cling to power, basic human rights being denied to so many and conflict causing such death, destruction and suffering, that we become angry enough to do more than wearily accept that this is 'the way of the world'.

But in complete contrast the destructive and misplaced nature of Cain's anger can achieve no good thing. It is the anger of one who believes that he or she should have got the promotion that another colleague was given and who never forgives them for it, the anger of the person in charge addicted to having it their own way whose authority is questioned, the anger of one jealous as others are praised, the anger of one who can't bear to lose (whether that be an argument or an election). Those who allow this kind of anger to become their master hurt other people in all sorts of ways and sometimes end up, as in the case of Cain, finding the intended or unintended consequences a profound cause for lasting regret.

It is worth noting that although Cain finds his punishment unbearable he is not as a result simply cut loose by God – indeed the 'mark of Cain' (v 15-16) protects him from the same fate as his brother (backed by the threat of severe divine vengeance!) It's a reminder that anger does have a habit of multiplying and causing a chain reaction. During the Covid pandemic isolating those infected with the virus played a key part in lowering rates of transmission and here God acts to isolate the sin of Cain and draw its sting knowing its destructive and replicatory force. The words of Jesus from the cross, 'Father, forgive them, for they know not what they are doing' (Luke 23:34) offer a radical response to violent anger; one that challenges all who claim to follow him to make a lifetime commitment to learning to love without limits. Making the immeasurable love expressed in those extraordinary and world changing words from the cross real and present is a sacred Christian vocation and means that, wherever and whenever we can, we are called to interrupt the chain reaction so often caused by sin, including bitter and belligerent anger, and make the wonderful possibilities of embracing the love of Jesus more fully known.

And if we examine our own hearts, we may find some misplaced anger lurking that we are often barely conscious of, but which surprises us from time to time with its vehemence. It might even relate to something that happened a long time ago and has never been properly addressed and sorted out. Such anger has the power to cripple emotionally and spiritually meaning that through prayer, good advice and maybe, if needed, professional counselling, we need to find a way of moving on. It is often in the letting go that the path to freedom and new ways of being are found.

Questions: Have you ever allowed misplaced anger to be your master? How do you think Jesus was able to forgive those who crucified him?

Prayer: Lord, forgive us when we become needlessly angry and help us to forgive those who have been needlessly angry with us. Amen.

Lot: Genesis 19:1-29
'Flee for your lives' (v 17)

It's important to keep in mind that this story is about xenophobia rather than sexuality. It is the lust to dominate that is expressed here in gang rape which, whatever form it takes, is brutal and humiliating. Lot's offer to defuse the situation and protect his visitors by offering up his daughters merely compounds the obscenity. Nobody comes out of this well, not least Lot himself who has a drunken, incestuous relationship with both his daughters in the next chapter.

It is significant that the later prophet Ezekiel says of Sodom that, 'She and her daughters were arrogant, overfed, and unconcerned; they did not help the poor and needy. They were haughty and did detestable things…' (Ezekiel 16:49-50). The things that happen in this passage reflect a society that seems primarily to have forgotten its obligations to the poor and vulnerable; one reason why it was extremely unfair to the LGBT+ community to ever associate them with the sins of this town.

Lot was Abraham's nephew and had turned up in the locality of Sodom, situated in the plain of the Jordan River, having separated from his uncle because of the danger of their combined flocks overgrazing. Although by the time this story takes place Lot had clearly been settled in Sodom for some time the locals have far from taken him to their hearts. His visitors, two of the three men who called to see Abraham in the previous chapter (Genesis 18:2) and here identified as angels, come with a warning that Lot needs to pack up quickly and leave town to avoid the coming destruction.

The desire of the citizens of Sodom to dominate puts Lot's visitors in grave danger. This desire, then as now, often exerts itself over 'those who don't belong' which is how their putative attackers saw Lot and his visitors. Their attitude has much in common with the kind of xenophobic fears that we recognise from our own day as the triggers for so much vicious and cruel behaviour. It's why in so many countries minorities have such a hard time of it and why migrants fleeing war and destitution continue to arrive in Europe (if they manage to survive crossing the Mediterranean Sea in overcrowded boats often not seaworthy) only to find themselves behind barbed wire or on the wrong side of a closed border crossing.

Jesus, in stark contrast, lived a life marked by love rather than fear. It enabled him to see people suffering from leprosy, a minority group shunned by those, including their own family members, who were terrified of catching it (which was pretty much everyone), as those who needed to be loved. Just imagine for a moment how it might feel for such a person after many years of complete isolation simply to be reached out to by Jesus. John in his first letter says that 'There is no fear in love. But perfect love drives out fear, for fear has to do with punishment. The one who fears is not made perfect in love' (1 John 4:18).

Of course, none of us is perfect, and we all know what it means to have fears and anxieties (for example those focused in recent times on the COVID-19 pandemic), and we sometimes struggle to offer love in the way that Jesus did. Yet the constancy of God's love for humanity is clearly and concisely expressed in words from Hebrews, quoting the book of Deuteronomy, '…never will I leave you; never will I forsake you' (Hebrews 13:5). We don't know much about Sodom; the town has never been found and we must assume that the destruction attributed to God in this story represents the memory of a catastrophic earthquake in a seismically active area. Yet as Lot and his family flee, God's mercy guides them, imperfect as they are. As we move from fear to love it is important for us not to keep looking over our shoulders, as Lot's wife notoriously did in this story, but to keep facing forward. As Paul puts it, '…but I press on to take hold of that for which Christ Jesus took hold of me' (Philippians 3:12).

There is an echo here of the storm on the Sea of Galilee when Peter, having seen Jesus walking on the water has a typically irresistible urge to join him. Having got out of the boat and gone some distance he looks away from Jesus and must be rescued before being overwhelmed by the wind and waves (Matthew 14:25-33). Whilst his focus on Jesus held, he felt connected to his love and power, but once he looked away fear that he was about to drown because of his foolishness took over. Peter and his fellow disciples would certainly understand the fears of those seeking to cross the Mediterranean at great risk to themselves; fishing on the Sea of Galilee was a perennially dangerous way of making a living! Jesus encouraged Peter to look away from his fears and see in his divine presence how fear dissolves into love. Living in a world in which fear drives everything from the way people vote to panic buying, we are called to keep our eyes on the love of Jesus. As she was escaping the place of fear and destruction Lot's wife made the mistake of turning back to focus on her fears rather than looking forward to her deliverance. Whilst every human being is a work in progress and the impulse to keep looking over our shoulders never quite goes away, if fear is to fully dissolve in God's love it is important that we do resist her temptation. Christians are called to be followers of Jesus which, almost by definition, means looking forwards rather than back. The bottom line is that learning to love rather than to fear is a vocation profoundly linked with the call to daily prayer.

Questions: Why is it that people sometimes want to control and dominate others? How would the world we live in change if people were more accepting of outsiders?

Prayer: Lord, forgive us all for creating so many divisions. Help us live our lives with open hearts and arms. Amen.

Hagar and Ishmael: Genesis 16:1-15; 21:9-21 'God heard the boy crying' (21:17)

Conflict in the Middle East is endemic, goes back thousands of years and shows no signs of stopping any time soon. The day before these words were written Eyad Rahwi Al-Halaq, a thirty-two-year-old unarmed Palestinian man, was shot dead by Israeli police near one of the gates to the city of Jerusalem. He was autistic, had the mental age of a six-year-old and ran away from the police, who believed he had a concealed weapon, because he was frightened.

The story of Hagar and Ishmael is relevant to today's ongoing tensions not least because according to Islamic belief Ishmael was a prophet as well as an ancestor to Mohammed and several important Arab tribes. The roots of the parting of the ways this story describes lie in a somewhat dysfunctional family life fuelled by the poor relationship between Sarah and her servant Hagar. It is Sarah, who instigates a complex sequence of events by trying to fast track the promise God had made to her husband Abraham, that he would be the father of many nations, by organising a biblical version of surrogate motherhood. She later laughs at the very thought that she herself could bear a child at her age; the strain in Abraham's extended family is clearly visible.

The fulfilment of the divine promise with the birth of Isaac doesn't seem to have made family life any less complex. At the feast to celebrate Isaac's weaning Ishmael, by now a teenager, starts poking fun at his younger half-brother and the die is cast – the tension boils over and, as far as Sarah is concerned, Hagar and Ishmael must go.

Whilst this acts in one sense as a cautionary tale about the dangers of second-guessing God's purposes and running ahead of them, the concern which God exhibits for Hagar and Ishmael and the promise he makes to them remind us that no human being should ever be told or themselves feel that they, 'should never have been born'. After Jesus heals the man born blind in John 9 (and in response to his disciples' cultural assumptions) he repudiates the very idea that the man's blindness was punishment for the sins of his parents (John 9:1-3) – nobody is any less beloved of God because of the circumstances of their birth or the failings of their parents. Every human life is sacred and Ishmael, notwithstanding his father's weakness and lack of faith in God's promise, bore God's image. The storyteller wants us to understand that God really does care for him and his mother; we are not asked to believe that they somehow don't matter.

Sarah's jealousy culminates in a visibly distressed Abraham sending Hagar and Ishmael, his wife and son, out into the unforgiving heat of the desert where, despite God's promise that Ishmael will be the progenitor of a great nation, he must have feared for their lives. It is in the desert, with Ishmael close to death, that God demonstrates that even if Sarah couldn't give a bean about them, he most certainly could.

God not only saves their lives but invests them with meaning and purpose. Whilst it is implicitly stated in 21:12 that those descended from Isaac are the focus of God's promise, Ishmael's story makes it clear that his covenant with Israel is not at the expense of his care for and interest in people of other ethnicities. In fact, the promise of God to Abraham in chapter 12 that he will be the father of a great nation is followed by another promise that, '…all peoples on earth will be blessed through you' (Genesis 12:2-3); a thought taken up in the latter part of Isaiah in which Israel's vocation is understood as being '…a light for the Gentiles' (Isaiah 49:6). Jesus certainly didn't understand his ministry to be just to the people of Israel and it was in part his refusal to be the kind of nationalist leader that many of his contemporaries believed the Messiah had to be that made them so desperate to do away with him.

Ishmael is regarded by both Arabs and Jews as the ancestor of the Arab peoples, something which takes us back to the killing of Eyad Rahwi Al-Halaq. The story of Hagar and her son reminds us that although as human beings we are capable of cruelty and insensitivity to those who are considered outsiders, God has no favourites (something Peter discovered at the house of Cornelius – Acts 10:34). With nationalism on the rise (and not just in the Middle East) the Christian belief that God sent Jesus to die for all irrespective of who they are or where they are from is fundamental and underlines the fact that racism and Christianity stand in opposition to each another on every level.

The story of Hagar and Ishmael also speaks of God's particular concern for the poor and the vulnerable; those who are not able to look after themselves for reasons very often beyond their control. Benefits in Britain have been inexorably squeezed in recent years causing mounting distress and anxiety to many (greatly exacerbated by the coronavirus lockdown) and Christians need to respond. This could involve buying items for the local food bank alongside our weekly shop, giving to organisations that work with the disadvantaged in society and/or volunteering to help with projects addressing the needs of those in our own communities. The former Bishop of Liverpool, David Sheppard, wrote a book about how Christians should respond to inequality which bore the title 'Bias to the Poor'. It is impossible to escape the fact that Jesus spent most of his time with the poorest of the poor, something that should continue to shape our outlook and our way of life as Christians.

Questions: As Christians what is it that gives our lives meaning and purpose? What might God be calling us to do in these unique and difficult times?

Prayer: Lord, you promised blessing to all people. As you bless our lives may we, by your Spirit, be a blessing to others today. Amen.

Melchizedek: Genesis 14:18-20; Psalm 110:4; Hebrews 7:1-22 'You are a priest for ever' (Psalm 110:4)

Melchizedek is a figure that we know almost nothing about – and that, as we shall see, is the point. In the three verses in Genesis 14 that describe his encounter with Abraham we learn that he is king of Jerusalem, referred to here as 'Salem', which at the time in which this story is set was a Canaanite city.

On a visit to Jerusalem some years ago I went to have a look at the somewhat controversial archaeological excavations taking place underneath the Palestinian township of Silwan funded by an association called Elad, one of whose aims is to move Jewish settlers into the neighbourhood. These have uncovered not only the city that King David built in the 10th century BC but also the remains of a sizeable Canaanite fortress dating back to the 18th century BC, a reminder that Jerusalem has a history stretching back many centuries before David conquered it and made it his capital (2 Samuel 5:6-10).

Melchizedek is described as a priest of 'God Most High' (El Elyon) rather than Yahweh; he is neither Jewish nor does he worship Israel's God. Melchizedek means 'king of righteousness' and it is significant that by submitting to his blessing and offering him a tenth of his booty (from his recent raid on those who were holding his nephew Lot as a prisoner – Genesis 14:12-16), Abraham is implicitly acknowledging the validity of both his kingship and priesthood.

The writer to the Hebrews makes the most of the fact that we know so little about Melchizedek. He uses the reference in Psalm 110:4 to the Messiah being '…a priest for ever in the order of Melchizedek' as a bridge to link Jesus with this mysterious king and priest. To be a priest in the Jewish nation you had to be descended from the tribe of Levi and the family of Aaron – it was your family tree that validated your priesthood. But even though we don't know who

Melchizedek's ancestors were or how he came to be a priest king, the writer suggests that Abraham acknowledged him as his peer (Hebrews 7:6-7).

The point that the writer to the Hebrews wants to communicate is that the priesthood of Jesus does not depend on his family background. In his lifetime it was still only members of the Levite tribe who had authority to act as priests in the Temple in Jerusalem (Hebrews 10:11) as they were still doing when Hebrews was written (probably a few years before its destruction in 70 AD). Jesus was a member of the royal tribe of Judah (Hebrews 7:14) which begged the question as to how he could be a priest. He sees in the unknown figure of Melchizedek the one who points to the real nature of Jesus' priesthood. Whilst Melchizedek obviously had a family background, we have no idea whether his priesthood was in any way hereditary. It is the silence about this in the few verses in which he makes an appearance in the Old Testament that is crucial to the writer. It is the fact that he is just there, appearing from nowhere and having his priesthood acknowledged by no less a person than Abraham that offers an illustration (and it is no more than that) of the kind of priesthood Jesus exercises.

So, whilst Jesus isn't a Levite, he can be a priest of the order of Melchizedek (Hebrews 5:6) because that kind of priesthood doesn't need to be validated by a family tree. This gives him the freedom to achieve something beyond the abilities of any priest who served in the Temple, which is to give his own life for the sin of the world.

The unknown author of Hebrews argues that the endless sacrifices that lay at the heart of Jewish religious life were a bit weak and useless, didn't work and have become obsolete (Hebrews 8:13) which is strong language given that much of the Old Testament revolves around the sacrificial system! But this new High Priest, one who, like Melchizedek, relies on his own greatness rather than who he was descended from, has once and for all become a great high priest, dying on the cross for the sins of the whole world and passing into heaven (Hebrews 4:14).

So where does this take us? One thing that the writer to the Hebrews points out is that Melchizedek was king of 'Salem' (Hebrews 7:2) which he associates with the word 'Shalom' meaning peace. So, in Melchizedek the writer identifies someone who by being both king and priest and with a name speaking of peace points us to Jesus. What Jesus has done as king and priest is to bring peace between us and God by dying for the sins of humanity. This is not because of any sense that he has changed God's mind; that God was angry with us but isn't any more because of Jesus' sacrifice. Appeasing the wrath of the gods by throwing them a victim is something more akin to pagan rituals and Jesus came to do away with that sort of thing. What Jesus does, by his death and resurrection, is to take into himself the totality of the sin, suffering, sense of alienation and hurt that fracture our world's vision of God and our own relationship with him and assure us that God does, and always has, loved us more than we could ever know. As the song puts it, 'peace, perfect peace, is the gift of Christ our Lord'.

Whilst some of this may seem a bit dense and somewhat obscure, the bottom line is that Jesus' authority does not depend on any human institution but comes directly from God. Therefore we can, with a vision unseen by the many heroes of scripture listed later in Hebrews chapter 11, prayerfully put our faith in him, even or especially in the kind of painful situations that the recipients of the letter, under the cosh for their faith, found themselves in. So, in the words of the unknown but particularly wise writer, 'Let us fix our eyes on Jesus, the author and perfecter of our faith (Hebrews 12:2).

Questions: What do you understand by the phrase, 'Jesus died for our sins?' What difference does the fact that God loves you enough to send Jesus make to the way you live your life?

Prayer: Lord, peace is your gift to us in Jesus, help us to share his peace in our daily lives. Amen.

Jochebed: Exodus 2:1-10; 6:20
'When she could hide him no longer' (2:3)

In the film 'The Prince of Egypt' there is a scene where Moses, grown up and a member of Pharaoh's family circle, discovers hieroglyphs on a wall in the royal palace that depict the slaughter of the Hebrew children from which, thanks to his mother, he himself was spared. Pharaoh Seti, with comforting arms wrapped around the adoptive son of his daughter, tries to reassure him: "The Hebrews grew too numerous. They might have risen against us. Moses, sometimes for the greater good, sacrifices must be made. Oh, my son...they were only slaves..."[1]

Actions justified as 'for the greater good' have led to an enormous amount of cruelty and barbarity throughout history, not least the murder of six million Jews by the Nazis in World War Two. Those who planned and operated the brutal death camps told themselves that their victims were subhuman ('untermenschen'), a designation first used by Klu Klux Klan member Luther Stoddard to describe what he referred to as 'coloured' (sic) peoples who he believed to be a threat to white civilisation.

The thread that connects Pharaoh Seti I, the Nazis and the Klu Klux Klan is an irrational and obsessive fear of people who are 'different'. The contemporary 'Black Lives Matter' (BLM) campaign is an attempt to educate people that every single human life, regardless of ethnicity, is of equal significance. That means that, in the words of theologian and activist Jim Wallis, writing in the context of the BLM movement, 'Appeals to racial fear, grievance, and hate are assaults on the image of God in others. Therefore, every act of racialised police violence, every family separated at the border, every wink or appeasement to white

---

[1] 'The Prince of Egypt': Jeffrey Katzenberg (Producer). Brenda Chapman, Steve Hickner, Simon Wells (Directors). (1998) The Prince of Egypt [Motion Picture]. United States. Dreamworks Pictures.

supremacists, and every attempted suppression of even one vote because of skin colour, is denying the image of God – *imago dei.*'

The experience of Jochebad, the mother of Moses (we know her name because of the reference in Exodus 6:20 to the irregular nature of her marriage to her nephew), reminds us that victims of the so called 'greater good' are often faced with terrible decisions. Her bitter experience in the teeth of an unfeeling and absolute supremacy echoes into more recent history in the context of the millions killed by the regimes of Stalin, Hitler and Mao Zedong (not forgetting the Klu Klux Klan bearing in mind that one African American a week was a victim of premeditated murder by lynching, between 1877 and 1950). The sheer weight of numbers makes it hard for us to get a handle on the fact that every single one of those millions was a person like us. They were people like Jochebad, in fact, a mother whose anguish was ignored and whose son so nearly became a statistic whose death would serve the greater good.

The act of placing Moses in a basket and entrusting him to the river Nile may well, in the mind of his desperate mother, have represented a 1% rather than a 0% chance of survival. It is certainly a story of beating overwhelming odds. There is no mention of God in the text of this story, but it is clear nonetheless, even as the slaughter of the Hebrew children went ahead, that Moses was being preserved against those odds as the future liberator of his people. There is an echo here of the story of Joseph, Jesus' earthly Father, being warned of Herod's plan to kill all male children in Bethlehem under the age of two (leading him, somewhat ironically, to find refuge in Egypt). We see this providence not just in Jochebad's desperate plan but in the persistence and courage of Moses' sister as well as the genuine concern of Pharaoh's daughter and her willingness to adopt a baby who was supposed to be a victim of her father's infanticide. In the Bible God's purposes are often advanced by the unlikeliest people, something we would do well to remember as we consider how he works in the world today.

Whilst this is a troubling story, it is important for us to understand that those families who weren't given what seems to have been special protection still mattered to God. Jesus may have been preserved in the early years of his life, but his mother subsequently had to endure the sight of him being executed reminding us that God identifies with all victims of the kind of hatred and violence which so often lie just under the surface of what Pharaoh labelled the 'greater good'. Modern day Pharaohs tend not to care much about anything other than retaining and exercising power over others, whatever the cost of that might be to ordinary people. But by sending Jesus to give his life for us and by allowing him to be the victim of those who were playing power games, God has shown that he empathises and identifies with the poor, the powerless, the victimised, the overlooked and the bereaved. Indeed, Moses himself came to understand as an adult that his place was not with the privileged and powerful people he grew up with, but alongside his fellow Hebrew slaves in whose liberation he would play such a pivotal role.

There are many mothers like Jochebed in today's world whose lives have been blighted by oppression, war, disease, and malnutrition which together continue to cost the lives of many adults and children worldwide. Whilst we can't do everything, doing something is certainly better than doing nothing. So how might we mirror in the context of our own pilgrimage of faith, in our giving and campaigning for example, this divine bias to the poor and persecuted that marked the life and ministry of Jesus? After all, we do claim to be his followers…

Questions: Why are we often afraid of people 'not like us'? Have we ever been helped by an 'unlikely person'? What did it make us think and feel?

Prayer: Lord, every member of the human family is made in your image. Help us to live our lives in the light of that truth. Amen.

Bezalel and Oholiab: Exodus 31:1-11
'See I have chosen' (v 2)

Back in the 1990s I took a tour round the (now defunct) Waterford Crystal plant in Ireland. I was very struck by the fact that becoming a glass blower or cutter (you had to decide which you wanted to be – one or the other rather than both – at the beginning of your training) required an eight-year apprenticeship. This sounded far-fetched but seeing the quality (and price) of the finished items for sale in the factory shop at the end of the tour, the immense skill of such expert craftspeople was on display for all to see.

It's lovely and very significant that the book of Exodus pays tribute to the wonderful God given skills of Bezalel and Oholiab. The Tent of Meeting, which they were so instrumental in beautifying, was a sort of mobile worship space that could be packed up and carried with them as the Israelites wandered around in the wilderness. It housed the Ark of the Covenant, containing the Ten Commandments written on stone tablets, and was the place in which the presence of God was believed to be localised: in that sense being a portable precursor to the Jerusalem Temple.

Bezalel, Oholiab, and their colleagues were able to fashion it into a very beautiful space which greatly enhanced the sense of God's presence within. They had a wide remit that included the decoration of the Tent of Meeting, the creation of the Ark of the Covenant, everything necessary for sacrificial offerings to be made and the garments worn by the priests. We can imagine them working together to create a wonderful space for the worship of God. It puts me a little in mind of the television programme DIY SOS in which tradesmen of all kinds; bricklayers, plasterers, joiners, plumbers, electricians, landscape gardeners and many others come together to give their time and skills to adapt the homes of families with specific needs who are not in a position to help themselves. In their hard hats and heavy boots, they are using their considerable gifts and expertise to create a space in which a family can live and thrive. Bezalel, Oholiab, and their colleagues clearly didn't have hard hats or hobnail boots and had to use far more primitive tools than their latter-day counterparts, but they still produced something of immense beauty that worked powerfully on those who came there to worship.

The church buildings we worship in, whether they are ancient or modern, were all built to enhance Christian worship. Stonemasons, glass blowers and cutters, carpenters, joiners, artists, needleworkers, candle makers and many other craftspeople have beautified our churches. In that sense they continue to minister to members of church families across the world who sing, pray, share bread and wine and have fellowship in them (when there isn't a pandemic). For instance, the art of creating stained glass is an amazing skill. Whether dating from ancient or modern times, it is there to tell stories and express profound truths in a way that words cannot. For example, the panels in the 13th century Sainte-Chappelle in Paris depict over a thousand figures from the Old and New Testaments reflecting the need for visual storytelling in an era where few people could read. But I also vividly remember being struck by a depiction of the astronaut John Glenn in Grace Cathedral in San Francisco, built in the 20th century, which powerfully symbolised the God given human yearning for exploration and discovery. Bezalel, Oholiab and their latter-day colleagues transcend words as they open hearts and imaginations to the reality of God's love and the transformation of humanity that results from responding to it.

We read in Exodus 31 of Bezalel that God had '…filled him with the Spirit of God, with skill, ability, and knowledge…' (v 3). A few verses further on there is a divine affirmation, with reference to Oholiab and those working with him, that 'I have given ability to all the skilled workers…' (v 6). Although it might be tempting to see gifts such as these as more natural than spiritual that would be a big mistake. Whether worship is taking place in an ancient tabernacle or a modern church it is not just the leaders 'up front' who use God's gifts. In Paul's list of spiritual gifts alongside such things as teaching and healing we find other qualities such as administrative abilities that on the surface might seem more mundane but are equally significant and precious (1 Corinthians 12:28).

Continuing this line of thought reminds us that every human being has been given gifts by God. And whilst some of them, such as preaching, teaching, offering pastoral care and leading worship as well as administration and creating stained glass windows, are specifically for use in church, there are so many more!

Some are gifted technicians, sportspeople, cooks, engineers, schoolteachers, doctors, nurses, designers, artists, plasterers, decorators, builders, cleaners, woodworkers, organisers, listeners, carers, encouragers, and gardeners, to name but a very few of many divine giftings. Everything we are and all we can do is a gift from God to us and through us to others. And the great thing is that each of us has something unique to offer. In an age that idolises fame it's easy to feel that we are useless and have nothing of any value to contribute. But Bezalel, Oholiab and their unnamed colleagues remind us that in God's kingdom there is no celebrity culture, and we can be deeply thankful for the many inspired and gifted people who work quietly in the background and just get on with it without asking for their names to be up in lights. What is it that you uniquely have to offer? It may even be something you haven't discovered yet!

Questions: Do we sometimes feel useless? What is the antidote?

Prayer: Lord, you have given so many gifts to humanity. Help us to use the gifts you give us for the good of others and the growth of your kingdom. Amen.

Jethro: Exodus 18:1-27
'The work is too heavy for you' (v 17)

I'm a big fan of Jethro! He comes across as pretty much the perfect father-in-law, full of wisdom and good advice. He had previously received his daughter, Moses' wife Zipporah, and their children back when things were looking dangerous in Egypt (v 2); a wise move given that Moses had got on the wrong side of one of the superpowers of the time. In our passage he visits the people of Israel in the middle of the desert at a time when Moses' leadership of the newly liberated community is under strain owing to the unsustainable hours and level of responsibility, as well as the not inconsiderable amount of grumbling about him that was going on. Leadership in such self-inflicted circumstances can be profoundly isolating and the danger is that it can lead to a growing inability to understand or empathise with those needing help and guidance.

Jethro, as a priest of Midian and an outsider, at no point joins the Exodus as such (he just goes home in verse 27), but nevertheless has a profound regard for the God of the Hebrews (v 11) and cares very much for his son-in-law and the people he is trying to lead. It is a reminder to us that good advice, loving support and wisdom are not unique to Christians and often come from outside our own community of faith (something to which we should be perennially open). There is an echo of this story in the Book of Acts as the apostles try to carry a similarly insupportable burden of responsibility (Acts 6:1-6) in attempting to balance preaching the good news (with all its attendant risks) with caring for the burgeoning Christian community. The crunch comes (as it always will for those trying to do far too much) when a row breaks out regarding the daily distribution of alms. The upshot is that the Apostles appoint seven deacons to look after the day-to-day pastoral concerns of the community meaning that the Peter and the other eleven can now focus entirely on the apostolic mission they have been called to.

Delegation is an underrated skill! When leaders try to do everything, it isn't only very bad for them, their families and often their health; it is also frustrating for the capable people around them who are not trusted with responsibility. Bezalel and Oholiab, who we were considering in the previous reflection, would not have been able to construct and beautify the Temple on their own; they needed many skilled and motivated colleagues to get everything done. The need to delegate holds true in every sphere of life including the church. Whether we are talking about the organisation of the government or the local branch of the Mothers' Union, leaders will thrive, and others will feel that they are being affirmed and valued when delegation takes place. As businesswoman Jessica Jackley puts it, 'Deciding what not to do is as important as deciding what to do.'

Having been involved in leadership in a church context for well over thirty years I have learned from experience something of what the issues are. Handing things over can sometimes feel like an abrogation of responsibility. There are times when it is difficult to let go and trust other people to do things that you feel – usually wrongly! – you could do better (or at least in the way you really want it done) and when we even feel a sense of 'what I am here for?' as talented others get good things done. The inherited shape of ministry in the Church of England was what we might call the 'bus' model. The vicar is behind the wheel, as it were, making the important decisions and doing the important jobs while members of the congregation sit in their seats passively. We have moved on from there thankfully! There is much more of an emphasis on 'every member ministry' in the local church and it has been wonderful over the years I've been in ministry to see many people take on tasks and ministries and grow into them (whilst bearing in mind that sometimes they haven't and that therefore leadership isn't about always getting it 100% right).

Those who took on responsibility as officials 'over thousands, hundreds, fifties and tens' (v 21), ensured both that more got done and that it was done better. It was not a moment of moral failure for Moses; it was a moment of liberation. With the new organisational structure in place, he was able to concentrate on the difficult and contentious issues that he was, with his experience of leadership, best placed to deal with. Whenever you get sucked into trying to 'do it all', whether you are co-ordinating a project at church, taking on responsibility at work, caring for a loved one or helping to run a group or initiative in your local community it is not a failure to feel overwhelmed and not a reflection of inadequacy to ask for help and share the burden. Like Moses, we are all human beings and therefore can only do so much. It is a real blessing to have wise friends, like Jethro, who are prepared, gently but firmly, to tell us the truth and, quite possibly, save us from ourselves. Remember God values us most for who we are rather than what we do.

Questions: Have you ever tried to take on too much? What were the results and what did you learn about yourself and God?

Prayer: Lord, you made us as we are, help us to accept that we can only do so much. Amen.

Balaam: Numbers 22:1-18; 24:1-13
'I could not...go beyond the command of the Lord' (22:18)

Do we go along with the crowd, or do we listen to what our heart is telling us? Do we 'follow the money' or do we focus our lives on doing the right thing regardless of the financial cost? These are the sorts of questions thrown up by the story of the somewhat enigmatic Balaam. He is depicted as a sort of professional soothsayer, a cross between a prophet and a diviner, on hire to Balak, the king of Moab, with the specific job of cursing the advancing Israelites who are threatening his territory as they continue their journey to the Promised Land.

In the Bible his subsequent reputation seems to have suffered somewhat as in the New Testament, both Peter (2 Peter 2:15-16) and Jude (Jude v 11) disapproved strongly of his 'cash for curses' mode of employment. However, today's reading, complete with talking donkey, represents an occasion when he was demonstrably unable to do his job in the way his royal employer required of him.

Balak hires him for the simple reason that he is terrified of the Israelites following their military victory over the Amorites. As far as he is concerned, if Balaam does his job properly, for which he will be extremely well remunerated, Balak will at least have a shot at defeating them (22:6). It sounds a bit like an ancient version of something called the 'speech act theory' in which forms of words in and of themselves carry out an action. At a key point in the wedding service the celebrant says of the couple being married, 'I therefore proclaim that they are husband and wife'. The words perform the action; the couple are now married (unlike in Gilbert and Sullivan's comic opera The Mikado in which if you say it's done you can pretend it's done which sums up much of the political life of the early twenty first century). So, in the same way, once Balaam has pronounced a curse on the Israelites, they are cursed – end of!

On the surface, it's a straightforward job – curse the Israelites and collect the money. The problem is that he simply can't do it. He is not an Israelite but nonetheless he starts having conversations with Israel's God which render him powerless to curse and therefore cost him his fee. Like all of us, he appears to have had mixed motives, which explains why, even after agreeing to go with Balak's men at God's behest, he then finds his way blocked by an angel – perhaps he had had second thoughts overnight and remembered the money on offer!

Following Balaam's conversation with his donkey (either one of the equine kingdom's finest hours or evidence that, whatever the historical core of this story, it has been somewhat embellished) and his encounter with an angel en route, he eventually meets Balak and fully and finally realises that cursing those whom God has blessed can't be done. In other words, he must do and say the right thing despite any financial misgivings he might have had. In Numbers chapters 23 and 24 Balaam's words of blessing are recorded for us and the message is unambiguous; if even a mercenary soothsayer who seems to be devoid of any moral compass ends up, for once in his life, doing and saying the right thing, how much more, as God's people, should we listen to his still, small voice when faced with difficult choices in life. It might well be that the course of action that God calls us to is very far from being the most financially advantageous, the least complex or the easiest. But when we know in the core of our being where God is leading us, we just need to do the right thing. This is not the same as being reckless and we always need to stop, think, and pray rather than rush headlong, considering what our sense of vocation (whether that involves a major decision affecting our career or a sense that someone in need requires our help) will mean for those we love and care for. But we are called to offer an alternative way of doing life to the one that obsesses over financial gain, ambition, looking good and finding significance in what we possess rather than who we are. Our spiritual health depends on it.

It's worth bearing in mind that Moses, not mentioned in this story as such but hovering over it as the leader of the people who are disturbing Balak's peace of mind, himself gave up a position of privilege in Egypt to follow God's call to set his people free. As Christians we need also to remember that Jesus lived with and ministered to those on the margins of society rather than its movers and shakers and brought blessing to many who were living without a great deal of hope. We are called to extend that blessing as we share his love, work for justice and peace, come alongside the broken hearted, give generously and pray for those in any kind of need. Framing our lives around what is advantageous to us without giving any thought to the needs of others is a road to nowhere. This will have implications for how we use the resources entrusted to us by God (especially pertinent to those of us living in wealthy countries where the divide between the rich and powerful and the poor and most vulnerable can be stark). It also has implications for how we respond to such things as the way global trading arrangements benefit wealthy countries and how the effects of climate change are visited most lethally on those least responsible for them. Let us learn not to be a curse to those who suffer because of our desire for a comfortable life and learn to be a blessing as we (with reference to the examples given above) buy responsibly and reduce our carbon footprint. It will mean some giving up on our part, but we do this seeking more fully to love and serve the one who gave up everything for us.

Questions: Why is the love of money the root of all evil? What might we need to give up as we respond to the challenges of climate change?

Prayer: Lord, help us when we make important decisions to do the right thing rather than that which suits us best. Amen.

Rahab: Joshua 2:1-21; 6:22-25
'She tied the scarlet cord' (2:21)

The journey from Jerusalem to Jericho is downhill all the way from nearly 2,500 feet above sea level to over 800 feet below. The abundance of water and the rich soil are two reasons why Jericho is believed to be one of the oldest inhabited cities in the world. It lies very close to the river Jordan and was therefore the first obstacle in the way of the Israelites as they entered the Promised Land after the death of Moses.

The story of Rahab involves an encounter between those practising what are reputed to be the two oldest professions in the world, prostitution and spying. The precise reason why Joshua's two spies went to see a prostitute is a matter of some debate. There are those who see a certain amount of ribaldry in the account and suggest that they went there for the most obvious reason. Others suggest that Rahab was also running something akin to a bed and breakfast establishment offering the spies a place to hunker down in an altogether more innocent fashion.

It may well be that Rahab was a widow and felt compelled to sell her body to keep food on the table and a roof over her head. Be that as it may she is an unlikely friend to the two Israelites, especially as they are enemy agents. She comes across as a resourceful woman capable of the quick thinking needed to get the spies well out of the way, deal with the king of Jericho's henchmen and make sure that she and her wider family are kept safe when the city is attacked. She's an unlikely hero.

Jesus' parable of the Good Samaritan, set on the road between Jerusalem and Jericho, presents us with another unlikely hero, this time out of his vivid imagination. Whilst a priest and a Levite, both 'good guys', skirt around the traveller lying there naked and half dead, a passing Samaritan doesn't just bind up his wounds but takes him to an inn and pays for his care. The antipathy between Jews and Samaritans meant that the sting in the tail for Jesus' Jewish audience is that the one they intuitively despise and write off as 'one of that lot' is the one who acts with compassion and humanity. So, for them to 'go and do likewise' (Luke 10:37) required a sea change in attitude as their inbred preconceptions and prejudices are profoundly challenged.

If we look at some of those we consider to be heroes of the Old Testament story we find they are also an unlikely bunch and include a boaster (Joseph), a murderer (Moses), a trickster (Jacob), a bully and a liar (Samson) and a schemer (David). Bearing this in mind, if we were to question Rahab's motives more closely, we might find that they were somewhat mixed. Word had come to the city of the military achievements of the Israelites and perhaps helping the spies represented an insurance card for her and her family. Yet she took an enormous risk in fobbing off the king's messengers; if she had been found out she would certainly have had to pay the ultimate price (as would her guests). That is why, even taking account of the undeniable fact that she lied to save her and their skins, the book of Hebrews celebrates her as an exemplar of faith (Hebrews 11:31) and the book of James declares her righteous (James 2:25).

The German industrialist Oscar Schindler is named on the 'Righteous Among the Nations' database held at Yad Vashem, the Holocaust memorial, on Mount Herzl in Jerusalem. He also makes for an unlikely hero. He was a philanderer who after the war abandoned his wife in South America. He was also a member of the Nazi Party who spent much of his working life trying to make as much money as he possibly could by fair means or foul. Yet at great personal risk he rescued and protected well over a thousand Jews employed in his factories who would otherwise have been sent to concentration camps and certain death. In the film 'Schindler's List', which vividly brings the extraordinary story to life, he is given a ring by those whose lives he saved bearing a quote from the Jewish Talmud, 'he who saves a life saves the world entire'.

I wonder how many unlikely heroes are woven into the fabric of our life stories. People who we perhaps found challenging, who we fundamentally disagreed with, found we had little in common with, were tempted to dismiss yet who, in some way, gave us something precious. These might include a preacher who we didn't necessarily warm to yet who said something in a sermon that fundamentally changed the shape of our Christian lives or the most argumentative member of our bible study group who comes up with an insight that was exactly what we needed to hear at that moment in our Christian journey. It might be somebody whose beliefs are very different to our own or whose lifestyle is morally questionable who offers us a kind word, some wise advice or genuine concern through which we recognise God's voice. We write people off at our peril!

Which brings us to another important aspect of this – Christians do not have a monopoly on guiding us, inspiring us, or witnessing to what is true. All my life I have loved the music of the English composer Ralph Vaughan Williams. Although he wrote quite a bit of church music and edited the English Hymnal, he was an atheist in his youth before settling into a 'cheerful agnosticism'. At no point was he a professing Christian. However, I find, for example, listening to his Pastoral Symphony, written as an elegy to the fallen in World War One (in which he had been a medical orderly on the Western Front), a spiritually enriching experience which brings me close to the one who suffered and died on the cross for me and for all.

Whilst it must be said that this not something in the conscious mind of the composer it is something I find in the beauty of the music. It is evidence of our having been created in the image of God to reflect a creative love that is written into the DNA of the universe. The thread that ties Rahab, Oscar Schindler and Ralph Vaughan Williams together is a common humanity. God's love is visible in all sorts of unexpected ways and through some pretty unlikely people (which we might feel includes ourselves) which means we need to keep open eyes and attentive hearts. There was plenty that was awry in Rahab's life, yet she was able to make the right call at the right time and recognise that the God of Israel is, 'God in heaven above and on the earth below' (2:11). We may be tempted to write people off, God never does.

Questions: What difference do you think the insight that everyone, of all faiths and none, is made in the image of God makes to the way we treat people? How can we make God's love visible?

Prayer: Lord, you are the Lord of heaven and earth; help us to be open to your love even when it seems to come from unexpected people and places. Amen.

Deborah: Judges 4:4-16; 5:1-9
'I, Deborah, arose' (5:7)

My imagination tells me that the time of the Judges must have been a bit like the Wild West. The very last verse of the book articulates this, 'In those days Israel had no king; everyone did as they saw fit' (Judges 21:25). The Israelites are now established in the land of Canaan but enemies such as the Midianites and the Amalekites are also about co-existing uneasily with them meaning that conflicts are breaking out on a regular basis. The people of Israel are also subject to a self-inflicted internal vicious cycle which might be summed up as follows:

- The Israelites sin against God and are overcome by their enemies as a result.
- They come to their senses and cry out to God for help.
- He sends them Judges (such as Deborah) to deliver them.
- They are delivered from danger and once again live in peace (until the next time!).

It is significant that one of the Judges that came to prominence and got them out of trouble was a woman. Deborah is introduced to us as a prophet and the leader of Israel at the time in which our passage is set. The story, as is normal in the book of Judges, involves a level of violence which doesn't sit comfortably in an age when we see the suffering caused by conflict regularly on our television screens. Deborah is instrumental in delivering Israel in a story that famously ends up with a woman called Jael driving a tent peg through the head of Sisera, the commander of the Canaanite army, an act which leads to the destruction of their king.

Whilst military strategy is certainly part of Deborah's job description, it also included regularly settling disputes between members of the Israelite community; something that Moses did during the wilderness wanderings. Mainly because much of it is, the Bible can come across as heavily patriarchal; the vast majority, if not all of it, was written by men and its protagonists are also mainly male. It sometimes feels that we struggle to hear a female voice at all. Reflecting on this, I am reminded that when I was ordained in 1983, less than forty years ago, all those ordained with me were men. It wasn't until 1994 that the first women were ordained as priests in the Church of England and the first woman bishop was not consecrated until 2015. As far as the rest of the Christian world is concerned women are still excluded from forms of ministry in many contexts. There is still a long way to go!

And yet Deborah is not alone as a biblical woman carrying leadership responsibilities. In the New Testament, the first witness to the resurrection of Jesus was Mary Magdalene, who is sometimes known as the 'apostle to the Apostles' because she was the first to tell the disciples that Jesus had risen from the dead (John 20:18). A careful reading of the Acts of the Apostles reveals that women were very much involved in the leadership of the church. In his letter to the Romans, Paul refers to Priscilla and Aquila as 'my co-workers in Christ Jesus' (Romans 16:3), meaning most obviously that they shared his evangelistic ministry and explicitly identifies Junia as an apostle (Romans 16:7). The evangelist Philip's four daughters all shared a prophetic ministry (Acts 21:9) and the establishment of a Christian community in the house of Lydia strongly suggests (to me, at least) that she was exercising a leadership role (Acts 16:40). When Paul wrote to the Christian community in Galatia he affirmed that, 'There is neither...male nor female, for you are all one in Christ (Galatians 3:28) implying that the social gulf in his time that made it a man's world in every way was not to be reflected in the life of the church in which all are equal in God's sight and where all, regardless of gender, are gifted by the Holy Spirit for all kinds of ministry. Goodness me, it's taking us a very long time to get a handle on Paul's radicalism!

The fact that these references exist in the Bible, written as it was over a long period of time in which patriarchal assumptions went largely unquestioned, is surely significant. Those assumptions, which have been unchallenged in most societies for most of human history, have still not been consigned to history, as the #MeToo movement highlighting the continuing abuse resulting in large part from them, has demonstrated. These assumptions mean that God is still overwhelmingly spoken about, written about, and addressed as male, as in 'Our

Father…' I wrote a blog post a while ago in which I used the word 'she' to refer to God and it was clear from the response that people still find this a difficult concept even though there are places in the Bible where female images are used with reference to God. For example, in Isaiah 49:15 God says, 'Can a mother forget the baby at her breast and have no compassion on the child she has borne? Though she may forget, I will not forget you!' It demonstrates the enduring power of patriarchal assumptions that need challenging at every level in church and society if we are to reflect the inclusive love of Jesus.

At a time when men were overwhelmingly in charge of everything, it was Deborah's wisdom and good judgement that led to her breaking the glass ceiling and assuming leadership of the people of Israel. In a world in which many countries have still never had a female leader I find that deeply significant. The Inclusive Church movement widens this out calling for an end to discrimination in the church on the grounds of, 'disability, economic power, ethnicity, gender, gender identity, learning disability, mental health, neurodiversity, or sexuality'[2]. The calling of Christians everywhere is to make that statement real and visible in the life of the church, and the time is now. We have some work to do!

Questions: What do you think Paul means when he says, 'there is neither male nor female'? In what practical ways does discrimination need to be addressed in the life of the church?

Prayer: Lord, thank you for the inclusive love of Jesus that reaches out to the overlooked and rejected. Help us to offer his unconditional love in our lives and churches. Amen.

---

[2] The Inclusive Church website: https://www.inclusive-church.org/the-ic-statement/

Jephthah and his daughter: Judges 11:29-40 'She was an only child' (v 34)

I'll put my cards on the table straight away – I have a daughter and this story makes me recoil with horror. It's not only that Jephthah's action in killing his daughter (for whatever reason) is morally repugnant but also that God seems to be involved. We may well wish that this story was not to be found within the pages of the Bible, but it is very important that we don't use nifty footwork to bypass these difficult bits and stick to the passages we like. However reluctantly, we must address them.

Jephthah had a difficult start in life. He was the son of a prostitute whose exclusion from the Israelite community was engineered by his legitimate half-brothers. Growing up and then being chucked out of a family and nation in which you represent by your very existence the moral failings of your father must have left its mark on him, constantly eating away at his self-esteem . However, the exploits of this mighty warrior and his band of followers had made a deep impression to the extent that the elders of Israel came knocking at his door when the Ammonites declared war (Judges 11:1-4). Jephthah makes the obvious point, 'you never wanted me around and you've only come crawling now because you are desperate!' and, perhaps because he has very little trust in them, insists on being put in overall charge of the nation (Judges 11:9-11). It is in this meteoric rise of a complex and troubled man that the seeds of his catastrophic error of judgement lay.

We pick up his story after he has sent a placatory letter to the king of Ammon which has been ignored. This means war and Jephthah's campaign is explicitly stated, uncomfortably to our ears, to be Spirit inspired (v 29). So why does he even make a vow that in the event of victory he would sacrifice the first thing that comes out of his house as a burnt offering? Did it never occur to him that it might be a member of his family, even his precious daughter? Reading verse 34 you can almost hear the storyteller weeping for this woman in the prime of life, especially in underlining that she was an only child.

I wonder if this is a case of somebody who approached a task feeling full of inspiration, thinking that the world was his oyster but who then took it too far and didn't stop for a moment to think of the possible consequences. I think, in a different context, of Tony Blair who, in his early years as Prime Minister had some brilliant foreign policy successes (The Good Friday Agreement and the liberation of Kosovo spring readily to mind) but then, possibly as an example of lost perspective, got himself caught up in the disastrous war against Iraq with its ongoing narrative of death, destruction and instability. Those in positions of leadership do need to look themselves in the mirror on a regular basis, even or especially if they are successful, and remember that they remain flawed, fragile human beings.

The story of Jephthah is a cautionary tale about somebody who didn't take the time just to stop and think and simply got carried away without considering the possible consequences. His daughter asks for a two month stay of execution to spend with her friends (very possibly it was a case of 'with anyone but my father') and, of course, there is the voice of another unnamed woman that we do not hear, that of Jephthah's wife, the unknown mother of an only daughter whose screams of misery and wretchedness remain out of earshot. In our world just as much as in the ancient world, the cries of those whose pain we would prefer not to hear, such as those whose children are dying daily of malnutrition, malaria or water borne diseases and those who are exploited so that citizens of affluent countries can buy cheap goods, so often fall on deaf ears.

I would imagine that all of us are familiar with the law of unintended consequences; we didn't mean for this or that to happen and if we could turn back the clock we would. There was, of course, no way back for Jephthah, no way of ameliorating the suffering his family had to endure because of his rash vow.

And where is God in all this? Well, we know that child sacrifice, common practice among many cultures at the time, was unacceptable to the Israelite nation; that's really what the story of Abraham nearly sacrificing Isaac (Genesis 22:1-18), an uncomfortable read in its own right, is all about. Having said that, another profoundly uncomfortable passage in the Old Testament law instructs parents with rebellious sons to take them to the village elders for the purpose of being stoned to death (Deuteronomy 21:18-21). The violence that exists within the Old Testament story (bearing in mind that Jephthah was a warrior who laid waste to twenty Ammonite towns, no doubt involving wholesale slaughter – v 33) is difficult and troubling, especially as we are made aware of the shocking realities of ethnic conflict on a regular basis.

So, although both Jephthah's sacrifice of his daughter and his slaughter of the people of Ammon represent standard behaviour according to the customs of his day, they are to us morally reprehensible and entirely unacceptable. It is in the light of the life, love, sacrifice and resurrection of Jesus that God is clearly defined not as a tribal deity who requires enemies (or daughters if they are in the wrong place at the wrong time) to be eliminated but as a God of love who requires us to love our enemies rather than annihilate them. God committed himself to the nation of Israel, even to the extent that he allows the 'Spirit of the Lord' to become identified as the military protagonist, not because he is violent and vindictive. The defining moment in their turbulent and tragic history, the moment this history is moving towards and would ultimately be defined by, was the coming of the Messiah, King Jesus, who, in an act of conscious non-violence on the cross fully reveals a God with passionate love for the entire human family, regardless of where they come from. Near that cross another mother, this time named as Mary, sheds bitter tears for the child of her womb, yet this time her grief was transmuted into joy and hope in the face of the Risen Lord.

Questions: Have you ever got carried away and regretted it afterwards? How did you respond and how did it change your life? How good are you at stopping and thinking before making decisions?

Prayer: Lord, forgive us when we act without thinking and hurt other people. Give us wisdom and right judgement in all things. Amen.

Ruth: Ruth 1:1-18
'Your people will be my people' (v 16)

A few years ago, one of my brothers sent off a DNA swab to get an idea of our family's ethnic origins. The result showed that while just over 80% of our origins are 'British and Irish', we are apparently 8.8% Iberian, 6.2% Eastern European, 3.6% Ashkenazi Jewish and 0.8% Finnish. The Iberian ethnicity is explained by the fact that between 4,000 and 5,000 years ago, a time when there were only a few thousand inhabitants in the British Isles, Iberian fishermen migrated from what is now Spain across the Bay of Biscay and are now thought of as the indigenous inhabitants of Britain. It is a reminder that every single one of us is descended from people who migrated here from somewhere else. Some of these migrations were for economic reasons (the Windrush generation), others came as invaders (Romans, Vikings and Normans) and others came as refugees, fleeing persecution and poverty (Huguenots). This perspective should profoundly inform and shape our response to migration today. The fact that migrants, many of whom never wanted to leave their homes but were compelled to do so by conflict and poverty, often find themselves confronted by barbed wire and the message, 'you are not welcome here, go back home' is both unbiblical and a denial of our own ethnic origins.

I write this just days after yet another family doing exactly what Ruth did lost their lives. Rasoul Iran-Nejad, his wife Shiva Mohammad Panahi and their children Anita, Armin, and Artin, having fled Iranian Kurdistan, drowned in the English Channel trying to join family in the UK. Ethnic Kurds are a minority group in several Middle Eastern countries including Iran. Every day they face discriminatory underfunding and those who protest about their situation are liable to find themselves facing arrest, torture, and death. Rasoul and Shiva wanted to reach Britain but placed their lives in the hands of one of the many criminal gangs who put people in overcrowded, unsafe boats to cross the Channel and don't give them another thought. They were desperate to find somewhere to bring up their children without the constant threat of violence.

We have all been made aware the dreadful conditions in which many migrants live, whether they have taken the decision to flee their home countries or, like the Rohingya Muslims of Myanmar, been forced out at gunpoint. If we want to read the book of Ruth and hear God speak to us through it, we will find ourselves unable to close our hearts to the urgency of the need. Naomi, Ruth's mother-in-law, and her family were themselves economic migrants as desperate as their contemporary counterparts to flee famine and poverty.

The opening verse of the book of Ruth provides us with its setting in 'the days when the Judges ruled' (v 1). We already know that this was a time of instability and constant conflict. Well, it was if we consider the stories of Israel's leaders anything to go by. The movingly beautiful story of Ruth reminds us that we mustn't overlook, in any society at any time, the stories of ordinary people trying to live their lives and do the right thing in difficult circumstances; another perspective to consider with reference to migration today. The picture of Bethlehem reflected in this story is of a place where people can find a home, look out for one another, and have sensible conversations when potentially difficult issues need addressing, such as, in this case, who will take the responsibility of a 'kinsman-redeemer' in marrying Ruth.

One important detail easy to miss as we read between the lines is that at the beginning of the book, they found hospitality and shelter in Moab (a traditional enemy of Israel), so much so that Naomi's sons both married Moabite wives. And following the tragic deaths of all their husbands Naomi and her two daughters-in-law share a moving conversation that takes up the second half of our reading. It is framed around the 'hesed', the loving kindness of God that Naomi wishes both Ruth and Orpah to experience. Whilst Orpah decides that she belongs back with her own people (and is not in any way judged for this), Ruth feels that she belongs with Naomi and her people. This sense of belonging goes beyond just living in a particular community. When Ruth says to Naomi that, 'your people will be my people and your God my God.' (v 16), she is expressing her total commitment to her new community. This is not saying that she would have been judged if she had not committed herself to Israel's God and is not therefore a proof text telling us that when today's refugees arrive at our shores, they should immediately adopt our societal norms wholesale.

What it is saying is that there is something beautiful about Ruth's loyalty to her mother-in-law and the deep love that existed between them. They are two women who both know what it is like to lose loved ones and leave their homes and in this conversation we see them exploring personal loyalty and what it means to belong in ways that change their lives. In the case of Ruth, it brings her to Boaz who goes the extra mile to protect her and eventually marries her. So, from what perspective do we see those who have had to leave their homes and communities? How can we seek to protect and provide hospitality to the most vulnerable members of the communities in which we live and the wider world we are part of? How can we express the 'hesed', the loving kindness of God, to those who find themselves grieving for the loss of home and family? We don't need to look too far for opportunities to be generous both with our money and our time. To give just one example, a retiring collection at a school carol service which took place annually in the parish church of my local community raised money for Save the Children (www.savethechildren.org) who have a dedicated fund to help child refugees.

Many people today, for all sorts of reasons, turn their backs on refugees and migrants as if it's 'nothing to do with me'. Followers of Jesus cannot do that because that is not what he did. He stopped at the gate of Jericho for Bartimaeus (who we will meet again later), a blind man who had been excluded from his community and was begging on the streets. In doing so he cut right across those who were telling Bartimaeus to shut up and go away and, in loving and healing him, Jesus demonstrated exactly the loving kindness we see in the book of Ruth. Jesus stopped; think about that. He stopped when he could have acceded to the crowd's wishes and carried on out of the city. We too need to stop and hear the voices of those, from countries such as Syria, Libya and Afghanistan, who are leaving their communities because their homes have been destroyed, who are drowning trying to cross the English Channel and who feel that nobody wants to offer them hospitality, welcome and a place to belong. In doing that we may need to think through how far we have come in overcoming our own inborn prejudices because those who end up far from home are, in an important sense, as much family as our own loved ones.

Questions: How have we responded to the needs of those who have become refugees? What more could we do?

Prayer: Lord Jesus, you yourself were a refugee in Egypt and know what it is like to have to leave home. Help us to open our hearts to the victims of war and poverty and help them, through the compassion and loving kindness of strangers like us, find, with Ruth, a place to belong. Amen.

Jonathan: 1 Samuel 18:1-4; 23:15-18; 2 Samuel 1:26
'You were very dear to me' (1:26)

The nature of the relationship between David and Jonathan has been the subject of much speculation. The statement that Jonathan 'became one in spirit with David, and loved him as himself (18:1) and David's words, in his lament for Jonathan following his death in battle, testifying to a love that was, 'more wonderful than that of women' (1:26) have led some, but not all, to conclude that their relationship was more than platonic being, in reality, a consummated same-sex relationship. Various aspects of the text have been adduced by commentators on either side of the debate and the reality is that it isn't clear one way or the other. What we can say without doubt was that there was a powerful bond between them that presents us with an example of a beautiful friendship marked by love and loyalty.

Given the context, their friendship was an unlikely one. One might have expected Jonathan, as the eldest son of Saul and therefore next in line to the throne, to have seen David, especially after his spectacular triumph over Goliath, as a major threat; an upstart with every chance of supplanting him as the heir apparent. As it happens that is exactly how his father King Saul viewed David. Yet Jonathan's act of divesting himself of his military uniform and handing it to David (18:4) and his explicit statement to his soul mate that, 'I will be second to you' (23:17) suggest that he saw David as the man to lead the nation and was more than happy to accept a demotion.

There's a resonance here with John the Baptist. When Jesus appeared at the river Jordan with a request for baptism, he was completely unknown whilst John, the greatest preacher of his day, attracted thousands of people who came out into the desert to hang on his every word. Yet John intuitively recognised Jesus as the one, 'whose sandals I am not fit to carry' (Matthew 3:11). Here was somebody who hadn't let it all go to his head and who understood that his role was to support rather than to be the main attraction.

Our contemporary world could do with a few more Jonathans (and a few more John the Baptists, come to think of it)! Modern Western culture has become celebrity obsessed to an unhealthy degree as fame and wealth are sought after as the way to a happy, fulfilled, and significant life; one that gives you apparent significance. The Hollywood actor Denzel Washington wrote of his successful career, 'Success? I don't know what that word means. I'm happy. But success, that goes back to what in somebody's eyes success means. For me, success is inner peace. That's a good day for me'. Washington is reflecting on what is most important in his life and for him being a successful human being is much more about the disposition of his soul than fame or the number of people who went to see his latest film.

Jonathan comes across as somebody for whom status and the trappings of power meant little and who was very happy to give way to David and do without them. What does this have to say to the person who didn't get that promotion at work they so wanted or to those, in whatever walk of life, who need to feel that they are in charge? The humble ability not to be endlessly self-promoting, to be happy not being number one, is critical in every part of society including in the life of Christian communities. In his letter to the church at Philippi, Paul encourages his friends to, 'Do nothing out of vain conceit, but in humility consider others better than yourselves. Each of you should look not only to your own interests, but also to the interests of others' (Philippians 2:3-4). This is quite hard to do as we are all subject to a very human tendency to see the world as revolving around ourselves and our interests, something that the society we live in greatly encourages.

Being a Christian is not just about filling our own lives with meaning, although that is certainly part of it. It is also about taking up the cross and following Jesus. Jonathan's apparent willingness to hand over all the symbols of his status as next in line to the throne (robe, tunic, sword, bow and belt) to David is an encouragement for us to sit very light to those things which may appear to give us status including the size of our house, car and bank balance; our seniority at work, at the club or at church and the temptation to look down on those we feel to be less clever or able than ourselves.

Jonathan was clearly both loyal and humble. The covenant he made with David was one in which he gave away the political power he had been brought up to understand belonged only to him. He was a steadfast, reliable and loving friend who cared less for himself and more for others. Jesus himself was the divine Son of God who, as Paul puts it, '…made himself nothing, taking the very nature of a servant' (Philippians 2:7) and in doing so gives us an example to follow. His temptations in the wilderness focused in turn on using his divine power to meet his own needs, render himself invulnerable and grab power. He rejects all three and chooses the road of humble service; a decision that will take him all the way to the cross.

At the end of the day, it doesn't matter whether we are top of the class, head of the department, chairperson of the society or running that project at church. None of those, of course, are bad things in themselves as such but they are not meant to define us. It is being made in the image of God that does that. It is in embracing this fundamental truth about ourselves that, wherever we stand on the greasy pole, we become truth bearers and truth sharers.

Questions: Why is friendship so important? In a society so concerned about status, how can we practice humility?

Prayer: Lord, as we reflect on Jonathan's loyalty and humility, help us to see others as better than ourselves and seek opportunities to serve. Amen.

Mephibosheth: 2 Samuel 9:1-13 'For I will surely show you only kindness' (v 7)

There is a long political history of those assuming power ruthlessly eliminating anybody who might pose even a potential threat to their newfound authority. It was this mindset that sealed the fate of Tsar Nicholas II and his family following the Russian revolution of 1917 (noting in passing that, although it certainly doesn't justify the slaughter of his entire family, Tsar Nicholas was himself no stranger to this kind of behaviour). There is more than a whiff of this in the air following David's accession to the throne. Saul's death whilst fighting Israel's perennial opponents the Philistines on Mount Galboa exacerbated political instability and David only became king following a drawn-out civil war between his supporters and members of Saul's family (2 Samuel 3:1). Jonathan, who died in battle beside his father, was not Saul's only son and his remaining brothers were not going to go quietly, which is why David, once his throne is secure, arranges for several members of Saul's family to meet a nasty end courtesy of a group of old enemies thirsty for revenge (2 Samuel 21:7-9).

Before the killing begins there is a note indicating that Jonathan's son Mephibosheth (who, as a grandson of Saul could have been seen as a potential threat) had been allowed to live by David because of the covenant of friendship with Jonathan we were considering in the previous reflection. It's an unusual offer to say the least – covenants of friendship notwithstanding, he was still a descendant of Saul and if David had followed the standard operating procedures of kings in the ancient world, he would have had him killed without compunction.

But he doesn't. Mephibosheth is brought into the king's household and given the honour, usually reserved for royal sons, of eating at the king's table. A cynic might suggest that this made it easier for David to keep an eye on him, but it does appear more than likely that this is a genuine expression of the importance to him of the dear friendship he had had with Jonathan. This is underlined following the slight wobble later in the story when Ziba, Mephibosheth's steward, accuses him of plotting to usurp the throne at a time of national emergency with Absalom's revolt in full swing (2 Samuel 16:1-4). When David arrives in Jerusalem and meets him his demeanour and willingness to let go of property that was his by right suggests that Ziba has been less than truthful in his accusation. Through it all David holds remarkably true to his commitment to his late and much-lamented friend.

David's treatment of the other members of Saul's family reminds us that when we read the Old Testament narrative, we need to be realistic about the dog-eat-dog world in which it is set. The brutality we encounter, sometimes understood to be at the behest of God, tells us more about their culture (to my mind, at least) than it does about what God is really like. It is in reading the Gospels and reflecting on events from Jesus' ministry, such as the healing of another disabled man at the pool of Bethsaida (John 5:1-9), that we see the divine nature much more clearly. Yet this episode with Mephibosheth seems to offer a ray of light and anticipate this clearer vision of God in the kindness that is offered, the loyalty it represents and the gracious way it is received.

An important aspect of this story is the disability of Mephibosheth; a result of him having been accidentally dropped by his nurse in the rush to get him to safety during the chaos following Saul's death (2 Samuel 4:4). It is a major reason why it is unlikely that Mephibosheth would have betrayed the one who had offered him home, hospitality and respect as he would have been all too aware that his disability meant that he would never have been accepted as king of Israel. This echoes, albeit in a different context, teaching in the book of Leviticus which lists a whole string of disabilities barring any individual, notwithstanding the fact that he could claim descent from Aaron, from undertaking priestly ministry (Leviticus 21:16-23). Afflictions in the ancient world tended to be understood as punishments from God which explains the whole force of the book of Job in which he maintains his innocence while his friends peddle the official line and try to get him to 'fess up'.

Let's return to the man born blind healed by Jesus who we were thinking about in connection with Hagar and Ishmael. Jesus says very plainly that his blindness is *not* a punishment from God for something he or his parents had done wrong (John 9:1-3). Whilst Jesus seizes this opportunity to demonstrate the power of God, when we cross check with the letters of St Paul, we find a man who is himself carrying a 'thorn in the flesh', very probably a disability and thought by some to be a problem with his eyes; a thought backed up by his words at the end of Galatians, 'See what large letters I use as I write to you with my own hand' (Galatians 6:11). Paul is characteristically open and honest about the distress this thorn caused him but came to understand (after much pleading with God) that his call was to live and work *with* the pain. The bottom line is expressed in God's reply to his cry for deliverance, 'My grace is sufficient for you, for my power is made perfect in weakness' (2 Corinthians 12:9). I find an echo here of my own struggles with mental health (very much a thorn in the flesh), something that reshaped life and ministry in unforeseen ways. Similarly, this was not a visitation of divine wrath and I feel enormously grateful for the unconditional and loving acceptance of me and my struggles by the congregation I served, through which God's ongoing call to ministry, complete with thorn, was affirmed.

The Church of England has committed itself to fully enabling the participation of disabled people in the life and ministry of the church. That includes those with any kind of physical disability as well as those, like me, who have had mental health issues. Being church should be about enabling all to feel that they can be absolutely who they are without feeling excluded or discriminated against in any way and understanding that God speaks with a unique voice through every human being.

Questions: Do you have a 'thorn in the flesh'? Have you ever spoken to God about it?

Prayer: Lord, thank you that you made us as we are and love us unconditionally. Help your church to offer a welcome to all as we live out that love in our common life. Amen.

Bathsheba and Uriah: 2 Samuel 11:1-17; 12:1-13 'You are the man!' (12:7)

It has been said that if you place someone in a position of high authority you see both the very best and the very worst of them. Having just considered a remarkable act of royal kindness, we come back down to earth with a very big bump as we consider David's use and abuse of Uriah the Hittite and his wife Bathsheba.

This story takes place at the start of the fighting season after David's army has left to go into battle while he himself has stayed in Jerusalem. From the roof of his palace, up the hill from the residential areas below, David sees a woman bathing. The series of events that flow from his lustful gaze involve adultery, skulduggery and murder and the storyteller accepts no excuses for David's behaviour.

Uriah the Hittite was one of David's most trusted soldiers, part of an elite force listed in 2 Samuel 23:39. The designation 'Hittite' meant that he was descended from one of the Canaanite tribes that occupied the land before the people of Israel arrived from Egypt but given that 'Uriah' is a Hebrew name he was obviously very much an assimilated Israelite. His wife Bathsheba was the daughter of Eliam who also appears to have been a member of David's S.A.S. equivalent (2 Samuel 23:34) meaning that they were members of a military family. So here the royal predator is having his way with a woman whose husband and father are away fighting his wars. The story does not say whether Bathsheba went to the palace willingly or unwillingly; the bottom line is that she would have had no choice in the matter anyway.

The story paints a picture of Uriah as decent and loyal and in no way deserving of the appalling treatment he receives. When news of Bathsheba's pregnancy reaches David his first thought is to get Uriah back from the war to sleep with his wife (for which David's instruction to 'wash your feet' – 11:8 – is a euphemism) so that the child can be passed off as his. However, Uriah, a professional soldier adhering to a code of conduct which he expresses in words tantamount to, 'I can't be sleeping with my wife while my mates are putting their lives on the line in battle' (v 11) is a man of honour and even when David plies him with drink he refuses to play ball. His integrity costs him his life; he is sent back to war and instruction is given to Joab, the commander of David's forces (via a letter carried to him by Uriah himself who is unaware that it contains his death sentence), to make 100% sure he is killed in battle.

This is very much a story of a king doing whatever he wants, whenever he wants to whoever he wants with no thought or regard for the fierce loyalty of those he is harming. It's hard to see it any other way than a disgrace from start to finish. The only mitigating factor is that when Nathan the prophet, using a parable with pinpoint accuracy, tells David to his face what God thinks of his behaviour, he crumples in a heap, mortified by the sudden realisation of exactly what he has done (12:13). His penitence is movingly expressed in Psalm 51 although even there, as he says to God, 'against you, you only, have I sinned' (v 4), we might want to add that Uriah, Bathsheba and the child that subsequently dies (2 Samuel 12:18) were also sinned against as victims of David's shocking behaviour.

It's very significant that this episode is included in the 'warts and all' Old Testament story and it acts as a reminder that whilst human beings are capable of great generosity, love, and selflessness, they are also deeply flawed. In the New Testament we see this highlighted by the thoroughly self-centred power play made by James and John (Mark 10:37), the betrayal of Judas (Mark 14: 43-47) and the complete moral failure of Peter (Mark 14:66-72). It is only in the entirely generous, loving and selfless life of Jesus that we see what a perfect human life looks like.

There are a couple of lessons for us to take from this story. Firstly, it is a prime example of the universal tendency for one sin to lead to another. Bathsheba becomes pregnant so David, to get himself off the hook, decides to try and fool Uriah into to thinking it's his child. When that didn't work, he took the nuclear option and had innocent, loyal Uriah done away with. Sometimes it is in covering our tracks after mistake number one that the really bad stuff happens as we try to move the pieces around the board to make it seem as if nothing happened. It's partly because we don't want to admit our weaknesses to ourselves or to others – we're often afraid to be seen for who we really are, warts and all. We're also afraid of the cost that we may need to pay in terms of our personal relationships, our reputation at work, in the communities to which we belong (both in the real world and online) or at church. However, some words of Henri Nouwen seem very pertinent.

'Mostly we are so afraid of our weaknesses that we hide them at all cost and thus make them unavailable to others and also often to ourselves.... I became aware of the fact that in the sharing of my weaknesses with others, the real depths of my human brokenness and weakness and sinfulness started to reveal themselves to me, not as a source of despair but as a source of hope'.

It is in acknowledging the gap between who we seem to be and who we really are that true repentance and new life flows. It is the experience of our failures (common to us all) and the recognition of them (which others around us can often see so much more clearly than we can) that healing and authentic humanity can germinate and flower both in our own lives and in the wider world of which we are all an integral part.

Secondly, we live in a society where the frantic need to have everything we want is driving us to a dead end. Bathsheba and Uriah were victims of somebody who had far more than they did but still hadn't gratified his desires. The parable of Nathan concerning the rich man with huge numbers of sheep and cattle who steals the poor man's one single ewe (12:1-4) is pertinent both to David's appalling behaviour all those years ago and the vast inequalities that disfigure the world in which we live. Consumerism is self-perpetuating; those who have much will always want more and never be satisfied. Given the fact that the world's resources are finite that will inevitably mean that this will be at the expense of the many who have little or nothing. None of us live in isolation; our choices will have consequences not just for ourselves but for others. They may be people we have never met or know nothing of, but we still have a responsibility to order our lives in such a way that our choices do not cost them the earth.

Questions: Can you think back to any major mistakes you have made in life? Have you been able to experience God's forgiveness? Have you and those affected been able to move on?

Prayer: Lord, forgive us for our mistakes, especially those we repeat again and again. Help us to acknowledge them, learn from them and be more properly formed in your image. Amen.

Omri: 1 Kings 16:15-28
'But Omri did evil' (v 25)

Today's passage briefly describes, in not much more than a footnote, the historically spectacular reign of King Omri. He became king of the Northern Kingdom of Israel a little less than 50 years after the split with the Southern Kingdom (which continued to be ruled by descendants of David) and reigned for about 12 years. In terms of the wider history of the time he was an extremely significant figure who was militarily successful and established a powerful dynasty. He also founded Samaria, the capital city of his kingdom (1 Kings 16:24). The "Moabite stone", discovered in 1868 at Dibon in Jordan by German missionary Frederick Augustus Klein (who became an Anglican priest and worked for what is now the Church Mission Society), contains these references to King Omri from a later Moabite leader, King Mesha:

'Omri was king of Israel, and oppressed Moab during many days, and Chemosh [the Moabite deity] was angry with his aggressions. His son succeeded him, and he also said, I will oppress Moab.'

Other Assyrian inscriptions reveal that the Northern Kingdom of Israel was referred to as the 'Land of Omri' and the royal dynasty as the 'House of Omri' for over a century after his death. Yet the reign of this towering historical figure is given just 14 verses in 1 Kings 16, nearly half of which recount how he came to power. The reason for this is that the history writers of the Old Testament are singularly unimpressed by any of his successes. Their assessment of the kings of Israel is based entirely on their faithfulness, or lack of it, to God and it's clear that from their point of view the most significant thing about Omri is that he repeated the costly mistakes of Jeroboam, first king of the Northern Kingdom, by encouraging the worship of idols rather than loyalty to God.

If we check out the only other reference to him in the Old Testament, it's clear that his name remained a byword for the evils of idolatry for many years after his reign. Micah, prophesying to the Southern Kingdom of Judah about 150 years later, does not mince his words and foresees ruinous consequences as he accuses the people of following the 'statutes of Omri' (Micah 6:16), clearly in context a reference to the worship of false idols. In a twist of irony, ruin did eventually overtake the Northern Kingdom during Micah's lifetime as it was conquered by the Assyrians who deported many of its people and brought the curtain down on its history.

The story of Omri reminds us of the perennial relevance of Lord Acton's aphorism that, 'power corrupts, and absolute power corrupts absolutely'. Omri seems to have been a leader who was extremely capable but morally and spiritually bankrupt. We live at a time when populist and autocratic leaders have come to power in many countries with their divisive messages often carried via social media. Some of these leaders have cemented their power effectively for life; Presidents Putin of Russia and Xi of China being two examples. I have never understood the obsession with power, but it seems to work like a drug, once you have had a fix you just can't get enough of it. But it doesn't need to be so; Nelson Mandela led his country whilst retaining his humanity and upholding a public service ethic.

Jesus never really bothered much with those in power (until he had to) preferring to spend much of his time with the 'ptochos', the poorest of the poor, made up of those were excluded from the rest of society, often reduced to begging. It was here that he nurtured the good seed of the coming kingdom. In an age where it seems that certain people have an entitlement to a lifestyle beyond the dreams of the vast majority, we need to shift our gaze away from the trappings of power and address, in whatever way we are able, however small that might be, the appalling injustices that scar this beautiful world in which all were meant to be able to live without want.

Part of the problem relates very specifically to Omri, the tendency of humanity to worship idols rather than the Lord of heaven and earth. In Omri's time it was the gods of the surrounding nations that subverted the vocation of his people to worship and serve God. As we see in the writings of the prophets this wasn't just an end in itself, as in; 'serve me and not them or else'. Turning away from the one who had liberated the people and created a covenant with them had disastrous consequences for the moral and spiritual life of the nation. Micah, referred to earlier, addresses a community which has lost its moral compass because it has lost touch with its foundational calling to be the people of God,

'Her leaders judge for a bribe, her priests teach for a bribe, and her prophets tell fortunes for money' (Micah 3:11). Money is talking so loudly it is drowning out the voice of God.

The idols of money, sex, and power, which all figure prominently in the Old Testament narrative, are still extremely voluble today demanding our attention and claiming our allegiance. As human beings we have a God given need to worship but we too often look in the wrong place which means that, whether we mean to or not, we set up idols that sometimes hide in plain sight. We live in a culture in which rock stars, sports stars, soap stars, film stars and reality stars are placed on idolatrous pedestals meaning that even the most intimate details of their lives are dissected in the kind of gossip magazines people glance through while waiting for a haircut. These are lent a significance that enables their worshippers to get vicarious thrills (the lives of many celebrities are rarely their own) before returning to the seemingly mundane and unimportant matters that make up their own daily lives back at ground level. We have become worshippers with an increasing addiction to and reliance on such things as social media which too often mean we spend much of our lives with our attention focused on stuff that either doesn't matter or is even positively harmful, such as the conspiracy theories of QAnon that are engaging certain mindsets in the United States (including some evangelical Christian communities) in very worrying ways.

What Christians are being called to do; what you and I are being called to do is to worship the Lord our God. This means that we put him first and define ourselves as those whose lives are focused on prayer, engagement with scripture, worship and service. This does not mean that we have to throw our phones and tablets away (although it might mean that we use them less) but it does mean that we make space in our lives and in our hearts to hear the voice of God addressing our distracted hearts and minds with a gentle whisper and a call to serve.

Questions: What does it mean to worship God every day of our lives? What are the marks of a life focused on serving Christ?

Prayer: Lord, we live in a society distracted by so many things that do not matter. Help us to shape our lives around our relationship with you. Amen.

The Widow at Zarephath: 1 Kings 17:7-24 'The jar of flour will not be used up' (v 14)

I have never found myself in a situation in which I didn't know where my next meal was coming from. When I go shopping the supermarket shelves are full and there is an abundance of everything. Yet all it needs is the suggestion that food might run short and panic buying quickly ensues; just as it did at the beginning of the pandemic. It demonstrates just how much we take things like food for granted. The World Bank estimates that there are 135 million people in the world who are facing acute food insecurity with the consequences of COVID-19 potentially almost doubling that total. It is also estimated that the war in Ukraine, the 'breadbasket of Europe', will increase that figure to 345 million.

In our reading today the people of Israel are suffering from a lethal combination of famine and bad leadership. Ahab, the Israelite king, aided and abetted by his wife Jezebel, is one of the Old Testament's premier bad guys who seems to have pursued a policy of keeping his religious options open by promoting the worship of the Canaanite fertility god Baal (1 Kings 16:32). Whilst the climactic confrontation between Elijah and the prophets of Baal is still some way off, the narrative is already building towards it by demonstrating that it is God rather than Baal who can both cause and bring relief from famine (1 Kings 17:1).

Poor leadership at a time of crisis can be very costly and Ahab's deficiencies as a king are exacerbating the suffering of his subjects. Elijah himself is miraculously kept alive (rather ironically by ravens, who are more often thought of as scavengers) and is then sent very specifically by God to Zarephath (beyond Israel's borders; today it is the Lebanese city of Sarepta) on the understanding that a local widow would supply him with food. But it is the provider who ends up being the one provided for. With her breadwinner dead the widow is down to her last few grains of flour and her last vestige of hope.

The miraculous provision of food whereby stocks of flour and oil remain at the same level however much is used is meant to remind us that whilst the effects of famine fall disproportionately on the poorest and most vulnerable, they are disproportionately closer to the kingdom of God; a community that great wealth makes it difficult to be part of (Matthew 19:24). Ahab and Jezebel, back in their palace in Samaria, would not have been going short but the storyteller is in no doubt that they were getting it very wrong and has some very harsh words for them (1 Kings 16:30-33). The principle that in times of economic crisis the most vulnerable bear the brunt whilst the wealthy grow wealthier holds as true today as it ever did. There is an uncompromising challenge for those of us living in an ostentatiously prosperous society which includes an exponentially rising group of people who are having, often for the first time in their lives, to choose between heating and eating.

The second half of the story, the healing of the widow's son, continues the theme of vulnerability. We are not told how old her son was but he was clearly not of an age where he could support her financially. Both the woman herself and Elijah (v 18-20) articulate the widespread belief that a death of this nature represented a judgement of God. But it is made clear in the fact that life returns to her son following Elijah's impassioned and physically manifested prayer that this is emphatically not the case. Her son represented, perhaps, her last best hope of being able to have enough money to put food on the table and his death turns out to be no more and no less than the kind of random tragedy which we still find so difficult to understand. I have found myself in numerous pastoral situations where people have expressed the belief that something very bad that was happening to them constitutes a divine punishment for some misdemeanour. It can very much feel like that, as it did for the widow at Zarephath, but Jesus came to show us that God's way of doing things does not involve dishing out random acts of retribution to those who displease him. When Jesus wept at the grave of Lazarus a window is opened onto the heart of a God who feels for and weeps with those who suffer.

The widow had reached the point where she felt her life was over and that she wanted to die – she had just had enough. Later on in Elijah's story he himself, following his victory on Mount Carmel and his subsequent flight from the murderous rage of Jezebel, reached his own nadir in the silence of the desert as he implores God to, 'Take my life; I am no better than my ancestors.' (1 Kings 19:4). For the widow it was grinding poverty that made her life seem worthless, for Elijah it was the sensibility that it was 'me against the world' (1 Kings 19:10). There are many other reasons why a human being might feel that life is not worth the bother; the loss of a loved one, a struggle with mental health issues, living with a disability, addiction to drink or drugs or the isolation that was forced on many vulnerable people as a result of COVID-19 (to name just a few). Responding to this acute despair isn't easy and pious platitudes do more harm than good. Much more helpful for Elijah was that his urgent need for sleep and food was met (1 Kings 19:5).

Whilst many reach a tipping point, sometimes driven by circumstances and sometimes by their own failures, at which they feel that they are worthless and their lives are meaningless, that is not how God sees it. This woman was not just poor; she was an outsider as far as the Jews were concerned, living in a part of the world where Baal was the main focus of worship. Indeed when Jesus makes reference to this story in the synagogue in Nazareth implicitly suggesting his ministry, rejected at home, will embrace Gentiles, he barely escapes with his life (Luke 4:25-26, 28-30). Jesus, in referencing her, insists that God is watching over her, which is exactly why Elijah arrived at her door. Whilst there is much about life in the twenty first century that eats away at our self-esteem and makes us feel devalued, our Christian faith insists that God does not forget us. If any one of us was the only person in the world who needed a saviour, Jesus would have died on the cross for us. He didn't just give his life for us as an anonymous member of the human race; he knows our name, he knows about our struggles, he knows the things that trouble us and offers us all a sacrificial love that is personal, cleansing, renewing and never ending. This helps us to see our lives, whatever our circumstances may be, from a new place and assures us that we are and always will be beloved children of God.

Questions: Have you or somebody close to you ever felt that life just wasn't worth living? Is there something practical we can do for a friend or family member today to express God's love for them?

Prayer: Lord, though we find it hard to love ourselves sometimes, thank you that you love us more than we could dare to hope. Amen.

Hananiah, Mishael and Azariah: Daniel 3:1-30 'Look, I see four men' (v 25)

Who are these three guys, you may well ask? Whilst Hananiah, Mishael and Azariah were their Jewish birth names, we know them more familiarly by their Babylonian names of Shadrach, Meshach, and Abednego. Along with Daniel they were born in Judah but after Jerusalem fell to the Babylonians in 587 BC, along with many of the great and good, they were forced into exile. They quickly found that there were opportunities in King Nebuchadnezzar's court at Babylon for bright young men and they undertook training which opened doors to highly influential positions in the king's service (Daniel 1:19-20).

However given that Hananiah, Mishael and Azariah were faithful Jews living and working in an alien culture with very different religious beliefs it was pretty much inevitable that they would come across a roadblock. It arrived in the shape of a ninety feet high golden image which, whilst it may or may not have been of the king himself, was designed as a very visible object of worship. Here the unstoppable force of absolute royal power meets the immovable object of strongly held faith; every single person assembled on the plain of Dura that day, Jewish exiles included, was instructed to bow down to the statue.

From time to time in our own day, on the news or in a documentary, we see members of ruling assemblies in totalitarian states on their feet giving the dictator a standing ovation. What we are not able to see is what these acolytes are thinking privately; they all know they have no choice but to play the part of sycophants to protect their jobs and their lives. So it was for Hananiah, Mishael and Azariah – they were caught between a rock and hard place whereby they had to choose between betraying their Jewish beliefs and disobeying the king's command.

Their loyalty to God led them to a fiery furnace blazing even hotter than the king's anger at their disobedience. The story of their deliverance from the fire which didn't burn a hair of their heads and the presence of a fourth (presumably angelic) human figure in the fire with them vindicates the stand they have taken and leads to profound change in Nebuchadnezzar. He, of course, goes the whole hog with dire consequences promised now for anybody uttering a word against 'the God of Shadrach, Meshach and Abednego' (v 29). It is worth noting in passing that the king has not become a convert following this remarkable deliverance, God is still 'their own God' (v 28).

In the list of heroes of faith in Hebrews 11, the reference to those who 'quenched the fury of the flames' (Hebrews 11:34) is very likely a nod to this story. However whilst much of that chapter is about those delivered by God from all kinds of trials and tribulations, it goes on to list those whose struggles did not have such a happy outcome (Hebrews 11:35-38) and where there was no miraculous divine intervention to save people from prison, persecution, isolation and death.

This inconsistency of fate for those whose faith leads to conflict with religious and political leaders continues in the New Testament. Whilst James is put to death by the sword, Peter is subsequently rescued from incarceration by an angel (Acts 12: 2, 6-10). This surely does not mean that Peter mattered more than James. Testimonies from the 260 million Christians persecuted for their faith today suggest the same pattern (or lack of it). Whilst some, either through their own efforts or with help from organisations such as Open Doors (www.opendoorsuk.org), have been able to support themselves and live in safety, others have suffered less happy outcomes. The week before these words were written 39 people were murdered in the Democratic Republic of Congo just because they were Christians. It is estimated that between 50,000 and 70,000 Christians are being held in appalling conditions in labour camps in North Korea because of their faith.

Whilst there are many wonderful stories of answers to prayers and an enormous amount of prayerful work continues to be done in support of Christians who live day by day with the threats of losing their jobs, families or even their lives, the hard reality is that not everybody can be brought into a safe place.

Hananiah, Mishael and Azariah, were denounced by their colleagues out of jealousy, no doubt, at their rise through the ranks of the government administration. Their answer after they were hauled before the king speaks volumes. They did have faith that God would deliver them from the fiery furnace and yet, '…even if he does not, we want you to know, O king, that we will not serve your gods...' (v 18). They were fully prepared to pay the price if on this occasion there is no divine intervention. There is an implicit acknowledgement here that God is not always at hand with a 'get out of jail free' card but there is also a loyalty to God that will face the consequences, whatever they may be.

In our own lives there may well be moments when the situation we find ourselves in leads to a potential conflict with our faith. We may not be taken off to prison or murdered for our beliefs but we might be ostracised, laughed at, marginalised, scorned or misunderstood. In our working life we may be asked to collude with a decision that, for instance, unnecessarily threatens people's livelihoods here or overseas or that involves, at the very least, being economical with the truth. It might be that saying no to something we know to be wrong costs a friendship or carries a financial penalty. There are some tough choices to be made sometimes and the consequences of doing the right thing (or not doing the wrong thing) can be unpredictable.

Hananiah, Mishael and Azariah remind us that loyalty to God has to come first and that our lives need to be shaped around our faith rather than the other way round. This will sometimes require much prayerful reflection; knowing what is the right course of action can be difficult to fathom and there may well be subtle nuances to take into account. There may be problems whichever way we look! Faith can be costly. Jesus not only gave up the joy of heaven but lived a life of service that took him inevitably to the cross (Philippians 2:6-8). Whilst Hananiah, Mishael and Azariah emerged unharmed from the heat of the fire, there was no divine rescue from the agony of crucifixion for Jesus; no legions of angels appeared to carry him to safety as he was arrested, tried, mocked, sentenced, flogged and killed.

Yet that was not where the story ended; if it was then all those who have suffered for doing the right thing, including Jesus, would have suffered in vain. It is the resurrection that points us to a hope that takes us beyond such things as fiery furnaces to the righting of all wrongs and injustices as God's kingdom of love, peace and fullness of life prevails. The writer of Hebrews has a vision of Christ at the right hand of God and exhorts us to 'not grow weary and lose heart' (Hebrews 12:3). Whatever difficulties, contradictions and costly decision making we may have to endure, our living hope is focused on an inheritance that, as Peter puts it, 'can never perish, spoil or fade, (1 Peter 1:4).

Questions: Have you ever experienced conflict at work or in any other context between what you have been asked to do and what you knew to be right? How did you resolve the dilemma?

Prayer: Lord, guide us when we have difficult decisions to make and need to know the right course of action. Give us the strength to do what we know is right. Amen.

Esther: Esther 5:1-8; 7:1-8:8
'If it pleases the king' (5:4)

Esther is notably one of only two books of the Bible not to contain a single mention of God (the other being the Song of Songs). In many biblical stories God is centre stage, intervening miraculously to demonstrate his greatness and liberate his people. Whether it's parting the sea or sending down fire on the mountain, specific and often miraculous divine interruptions dot the narrative. But there is none of that in the book of Esther. Hadassah, also known as Esther, was a member of the Jewish diaspora living in Persia somewhere around the middle of the 5th century BC. When this story was set, long after Jews had been permitted to return from exile, significant numbers of Jewish communities continued to exist around the Persian Empire.

However Esther and her people had not lost their distinctive Jewish identity and her story revolves around a problem that is still with us today – anti-Semitism. There is much about the background to this story that is actually pretty repulsive. The six month long celebration of the king's wealth followed by a seven day booze up reflects a society marked by ostentation and over indulgence. The treatment of women reflected here, which included statutory rape by the emperor Xerxes as a means of selecting a new wife (Esther 2:12-14), is quite appalling. The planned liquidation of the Jewish community proposed by the senior royal official Haman fills us with horror; his plan to use their money to fill the royal coffers (waved airily through by the king as he hands the Jews over to Haman and his death squads) echoes chilling images of the Holocaust. In this society the king has absolute power; he can get drunk as often as he likes, bed as many young girls as he wishes and kill as many people as he wants without compunction.

As Esther and her relative Mordecai hatch a plan to save the Jewish community there are no big miracles in evidence, nor is there any confessing of sin and turning back to God. There is actually very little prayer and worship at all in this book (although the fasting Esther orders in chapter 4:15-16 could be interpreted as a way of turning to God to offer the situation to him). This is about how people in a very desperate and dangerous situation think quickly, take the initiative and undertake major risks to find a way to survive.

This brings us to our two passages for today. When the dreadful edict is issued Esther is instructed to make a personal appeal to the king as the only way to give her people any chance of avoiding annihilation. But the stakes are high; the almost universal penalty for anyone who approached the king unsummoned was death. We can only guess at her feelings as she stands unbidden before the king and at the depth of her relief as he holds out the golden sceptre meaning that, against the odds, her life will be spared and her request considered (5:1-2).

Because Esther was prepared to stick her neck out (almost literally) the king's edict is cancelled and the Jews are spared (as the second passage for today relates). Yet, while it is in one sense providential that she was in the right place at the right time, she was only there because she was, in effect, just one of many very young female victims of a king who treated women as little more than sex slaves. There was little chance, in all probability, for her to have taken the kind of moral stance demonstrated by Hananiah, Mishael and Azariah. No doubt she would have felt compromised and afraid (her role as the king's wife was precarious as her predecessor Queen Vashti well understood; Esther 1:19) and that this was not the life she would have chosen for herself. But she was where she was and she made the most of her situation to be, in effect, the rescuer of her people. In spite of all that had happened to her, deep inside her loyalty remained intact. She was, in more ways than one, a survivor.

There are times when we feel we are not where we wish we were in life. Alongside all the good stuff that we've been involved with and which has shaped our lives, all our stories also contain their fair share of wrong turns, difficult moments and times when we have both been let down by others and let ourselves and others down. Many of us, in one way or another, have a somewhat chequered history. Yet often unrecognised, God has been walking with us even or especially through the times when life has been challenging for whatever reason. Esther's story assures us that God is not distracted or somewhere else, but is close to us exactly where we are and as we are today (even if that is not really where we want to be) and waits to offer us new hopes and possibilities.

God never gives up; even though the world has more than its fair shares of inequalities and injustices, God is still offering humanity new possibilities which require us to identify where God is at work and to get involved. We're not asked to sit around waiting for God to pile in with a big miracle. We, like Esther, are asked to discern the times, think on our feet, sometimes take risks and remain loyal to God.

No situation is too bleak and awful for God to be present and at work even when the outcome is not as felicitous as it was for the Jews of Esther's time. The following prayer was written on a wall anonymously at Ravensbruck Concentration Camp during World War Two. It speaks of God's active presence in a hell on earth and bears witness to a beautiful and astonishing ability to forgive in the face of a level of murderous hatred that resulted in the death of millions:

'O Lord, remember not only the men and women of goodwill, but also those of ill will. But do not remember all the suffering they have inflicted upon us. Remember the fruits we bought, thanks to this suffering: our comradeship, our loyalty, our humility, the courage, the generosity, the greatness of heart which has grown out of this; and, when they come to judgement, let all the fruits that we have borne be their forgiveness. Amen.'

This, of course, places the revenge that the Jews took (Esther 9:5f) against those who had plotted their liquidation in the story of Esther in context; Jesus asks us to love and pray for our enemies rather than destroy them (Matthew 5:44). As Christians we are, like Esther, trying to be loyal to the truth as we understand it in a culture which is increasingly alien. As Christianity is being relentlessly pushed to the margins in our society, we face tough choices as we try to live out our faith as the tide of secularism comes inexorably in. Yet God himself can never be pushed to the margins no matter how it may look. In Ephesians Paul talks of, '…one God and Father of all, who is over all and through all and in all' (Ephesians 4:6) meaning that as in Esther's story God is perpetually present, sometimes in hidden and silent ways, in our lives and the life of the planet earth. Her story reminds that, in whatever way we apprehend it, God is simply and mysteriously there and offers us, wherever we happen to be in life (whether that be good, bad, indifferent, could be better, could be worse, still coming up for air after the pandemic etc.), hope and a future.

Questions: Are you where you want to be in life today? What possibilities might God be offering you?

Prayer: Lord, meet us where we are in life and show us the way you want us to go and who you want us to be. Amen.

Haggai: Haggai 1:1-11
'Because of my house, which remains a ruin' (v 9)

Have you ever looked forward to something which turned out to be a bit of a disappointment? It may have been a holiday that wasn't all it was cracked up to be, a show that didn't quite have the spark you were expecting or a new job that promised more than it delivered. Imagine the people of Judah returning to Jerusalem after many decades of exile during which they dreamed about but saw no possibility of going home. Even those who were born and grew up in exile would have had the city and its Temple as it was before the exile described to them vividly by their elders. As those making the journey set out for Jerusalem there would have been a certain amount of trepidation but also great anticipation; even though many of them had never been there, they were going home. The reality when they got there, of course, was a ruined Temple, a destroyed city and broken down walls. It would have been a scene of devastation and there was much hard and laborious work to be done before any glory could return!

The short book of the prophet Haggai can be dated precisely to 520 BC, a little less than 20 years after the return from exile. From the start there were major challenges exacerbated by local opposition (described in the books of Ezra and Nehemiah) and I suspect there were many moments when, rather like the Israelites of Moses' time dreaming of the flesh pots of Egypt whilst enduring the heat of the desert, the returnees ached to be back in Babylon.

Haggai's problem was with the priorities of those rebuilding the city. Whilst people had been rebuilding their homes and actually making them very comfortable, work on building the Temple, the symbol of the nation's identity as the people of God, had not even begun (v 2). Now in one sense it seems perfectly understandable that the need to house people was made a priority; Jerusalem is a hill city and can be cold in winter. But it seems that a situation had been reached where it kept on being kicked into the long grass. From this perspective Haggai's words are a call to action and a challenge to the people to get their priorities sorted out. One result of the fact that people are looking first and foremost to their own wants is that they are spending considerable amounts of money on unnecessary items (v 6b). Haggai pronounces that this self-orientated lifestyle will have consequences (v 10–11); economic disaster is on the horizon because the people have still not learned their lesson in spite of all their years in exile.

During the Coronavirus pandemic we spent many months exiled from much of what makes up our day to day lives in normal times as many of us were separated from our families and friends for long periods. Many families who suffered the loss of loved ones had to face the acute distress of not being able to see or say goodbye to them before they died. Many people were unable to go to work and worked from home, were placed on furlough or even lost their jobs altogether. Doing something as ordinary and everyday as meeting friends for coffee and a catch up was illegal. A considerable number of us spent the vast majority if not all our time at home.

So the return to normality (more or less) has been a little bit like a return from exile. We may feel that, whilst the exile in Babylon described in the Bible was a result of major errors on the part of the people of Judah, the pandemic was just 'something that happened'. Yet there is a potential link between the pandemic and the continued destruction of wildlife habitats which is placing humans and animals in closer proximity than they were intended to be thereby creating a far higher possibility of the transference of 'zoonotic' diseases (diseases existing in animals that can evolve to affect humans) such as COVID-19. Whilst I certainly wouldn't call the pandemic a judgement from God (it would be very strange to think of a loving God deliberately targeting the elderly and most vulnerable), it may well be a consequence of the careless way that we are draining the earth's resources and destroying habitats in our relentless desire to have more of everything. Haggai's words about consuming but never being satisfied (v 6) seem awfully relevant to our situation.

Haggai's words are remarkably applicable to our consumer orientated world; we also have holes in our purses yet our profligacy and love of things we want but don't need threaten the future of the planet. You simply cannot have unlimited growth on a planet with limited resources. That is why I am hoping that as we emerge from the pandemic we don't just go back to 'normal' but move instead to a new normal in which humanity can seriously address the threats posed by climate change, habitat destruction and global consumerism. That will require a profound change of mind for us all.

This is a vast topic and so it would perhaps be best to offer a few specific thoughts about food, drink and clothes, the aspects of thoughtless consumerism that Haggai focuses on in verse 6 of our passage. We should be prepared to ask difficult questions about how what we eat, drink or wear has been produced all the way down the supply chain to those who grew, harvested, picked and packaged what we buy. Are those at the bottom of the chain working in a safe, clean and fair environment (bearing in mind the Rana Plaza collapse in Dhaka in 2013 which killed 1,134 clothing workers employed by a company with links to a significant number of British clothing retailers who had been ordered to come to work on pain of losing a month's wages even though it was known the building was unsafe)? Are they being paid a fair wage for their labour? Are farmers and other suppliers being paid a fair price for what they produce (whether they live in developing countries or the U.K.)? Is the purchase we are making contributing to the destruction of rainforests and/or animal habitats? What is the carbon footprint of what we buy (some producers are beginning to introduce carbon footprint labelling)? Do we already have enough of what we are purchasing and how much does impulse buying play a part in our consumption? Are we reusing plastic bags and trying to reduce the goods we buy with unnecessary plastic wrapping?

If you (or a family member or friend) have internet access 'Ethical Consumer' (www.ethicalconsumer.org), an independent not-for-profit website which works with a number of organisations including Christian Aid, provides a lot of helpful information on the moral implications of purchases across a wide range of goods and services that we use as consumers.

One thing we can say for sure is that Haggai is seriously challenging us, along with his contemporaries, to purchase less and give more in order to arrive at a new normal. For him, prioritising personal comfort at the expense of rebuilding the Temple symbolised the uncomfortable reality that the people had yet again drifted away from God. In the same way prioritising personal comfort in a needy world today cannot be right; Haggai would certainly have a word or two to say about that! Profound change is required and Christians need to be at the heart of it.

Questions: As Christians what changes do we need to make in the way we use the earth's limited resources? How do you think future generations will assess us as custodians of the planet?

Prayer: Lord, open our hearts that we may reflect a spirit of generosity in all aspects of our lives including in the way we consume the precious resources of the earth that you have created and asked us to look after. Amen.

Joseph: Matthew 1:18-25
'Joseph her husband was a righteous man' (v 19)

In the course of parish ministry I attended many nativity plays in schools and churches. Understandably they don't tend to focus on the apparently scandalous event at the heart of the story – that Mary is pregnant and Joseph is not the father. It would be fair to say that while Luke's account of the birth of Jesus portrays Mary's perspective, Matthew gives us more than a hint of what was going through Joseph's mind as he experiences the roller coaster ride of Mary's pregnancy.

When Joseph discovered that Mary was expecting a child, Matthew tells us that he 'considered this' (v 20). We might well ask what this involved. The Greek word used, 'enthymeomai', suggests that he did this with more than a little emotional force. To start with, the penalty for what he understood Mary's actions to be in being unfaithful to him as her betrothed was death by stoning (Deuteronomy 22:23-24) – according to the Law of Moses, her life was forfeit. Added to this, of course, was his personal sense of betrayal; how could Mary have done this? We can imagine the anger, confusion and disappointment circling around in his mind endlessly coalescing into the same thought; 'I just don't understand!" Joseph was not some kind of superhero able to rise above such thoughts; he was a flesh and blood human being whose life at this precise moment was falling apart at the seams because of a scandal he thought he would never live down. It is to his enormous credit that his intuitive response does not concern how he might take revenge according to the letter of the law but how he can save Mary's life and reputation (v 19).

This begs the question as to why the angel came to see Mary alone rather than with Joseph. Why was he excluded from the decision making process? There isn't a definitive answer to this question yet I would tentatively suggest that in a stiflingly patriarchal society in which all important decisions were taken by men, there is a divine marker being put down in that this most significant of choices was Mary's to make. If we consider another Mary standing outside the tomb of Jesus and being the first to meet the risen Lord we can see that the life of Jesus is bookended with stories about the emancipation of women. For the church this profoundly challenges the exclusion of women from ordained ministry that is only now being meaningfully addressed and is still not a reality in every church tradition two thousand years on.

Joseph really comes into his own after he has his own angelic encounter in the course of a dream in which the astonishing truth of the matter is explained to him (v 20–23). He will have realised firstly that Mary, against all the odds, has not betrayed him but also that absolutely nobody else is going to believe that. 'Do not be afraid', says the angel to Joseph. There will be misunderstanding, ribaldry even (I wonder if and for how long 'Joseph and Mary' jokes did the rounds in Nazareth) and a very uncertain future but Joseph is prepared to do the right thing rather than the expected thing. We can imagine comments along the lines of, 'Joseph, what are you doing, you're out of your mind!' coming his way. But he knows the will of God and responds obediently. It's why he and Mary end up on the road to Bethlehem together.

Whilst Joseph's call to obedience in being loyal to a woman with child by the Holy Spirit is pretty unique, our walk with Christ will sometimes involve doing the right thing rather than the expected thing because there are times when they clash. St Francis was born into a family of wealthy cloth merchants who lived a life of luxury and in his youth had something of a reputation as a party animal. Yet a period of imprisonment following a battle he was involved in led to profound change as he embraced poverty and simplicity in a way that still inspires people today (highlighted by the decision made in 2013 by Jorge Mario Bergoglio to adopt Francis as his papal name). Yet at the time Francis's actions seemed inexplicable to those around him and, indeed, at one point he was dragged home by his father and locked in a storeroom.

There will be times when, as Christians, we are called to do things that will involve both a challenge to our own received wisdom as well as the possibility of being seriously misunderstood by others. Perhaps that's why Jesus rather ruefully reflected that 'prophets are not accepted in their home towns' (Luke 4:24). The first of these is a reminder that we will never have more than a provisional understanding of who God is and what his will for our lives might be. Just as the disciples needed to undergo a major cultural shift in embracing Gentiles as part of the Christian community, so our Christian pilgrimage sometimes involves putting what we think we know about ourselves and God to one side. This means that Christians shouldn't get too comfy – seeing faith with new eyes means being perennially open to previously unimagined ways of serving Christ. The second is a reminder that when we do follow Christ with all our hearts we may speak and act in ways that don't sit comfortably with everybody. I'm not talking here about deliberately winding people up or the kind of nonsensical and dangerous conspiracy theories that have taken root in some Christian communities in the United States in recent years. It might just be that our thoughts, words and actions won't always be fully comprehensible to everyone who adopts the cultural norms of early twenty first century society and therefore following Jesus may be costly in terms of reputation and relationships (bearing in mind as we have in earlier studies that the act of following Christ in some countries means putting your life at risk).

The relationship between Joseph and his peers would never have been quite the same after his decision to stick with the woman who had apparently humiliated him in the most public way possible. Yet, although he has only a couple of brief appearances in the Bible, Joseph had a hugely formative role in the life of his adopted son Jesus. I first visited the ancient ruins of the town of Sepphoris, seven miles from Nazareth, back in 2013 on my first pilgrimage to the Holy Land. At first, I wondered what we were doing there as the town makes no appearance in the New Testament. Yet among the ruins, there is a road, dating from the first century, along which Joseph and Jesus would have walked many times together. As the nearest town to the village of Nazareth they would have gone there together often to buy supplies and very possibly to do jobs as part of their carpentry business. It may be that the first time they went together Joseph carried his small boy on his back showing him the sights and sounds. We know that Joseph was still living when Jesus was twelve years old (Luke 2:41-52) but had died by the time Jesus began his ministry. God entrusted his Son to this loyal, generous, thoughtful and just man who helped lay the foundations of Jesus' ministry by his commitment to following God's will whatever the cost. We don't have to be centre stage to make a difference. Even the smallest act of service can lead to unimagined healing and hope. Whilst not everyone will always 'get' our motives as followers of Jesus, we can take Joseph as an example of what it means to put our faith first and foremost and to live it out day by day.

Questions: Why do we sometimes struggle to do God's will? How do we respond when our loyalty to Christ causes complications or misunderstandings in some area of our lives?

Prayer: Lord, thank you for Joseph's ability to accept your will for his life. Help us in our daily lives to do what is right even when we don't understand what's going on. Amen.

Simeon: Luke 2:25-35
'My eyes have seen your salvation' (v 30)

Waiting can be a real pain! It's something that we are less and less used to, especially when it's now possible to order something from the internet and have it delivered within the hour. We tend to regard time spent waiting as time wasted. However the writer Sue Monk Kidd offers us a very different perspective when she says, 'I had tended to view waiting as mere passivity. When I looked it up in my dictionary however, I found that the words passive and passion come from the same Latin root. Waiting is both passive and passionate. It's a vibrant, contemplative work.' Her words are particularly helpful as we consider Simeon. Having understood that his life would not end until he had seen the promised Messiah, are we to think that he spent his time twiddling his thumbs until he showed up? I think not.

His was a passionate, vibrant kind of waiting rather than the kind of waiting that ends up with us losing the will to live. His life was defined by his openness to the Holy Spirit (v 25–26) and when the Spirit is at work life is rarely boring. It's not stated explicitly, but his act of blessing Joseph, Mary and Jesus (v 34) suggests that Simeon was a Temple priest, further emphasising that his was an active rather than a passive waiting. His was a patient hope which endured as he lived day to day life with all its light and shade, times of busyness and rest, of health and sickness, of stress and calm.

Not only did his passionate waiting shape his own life; his ardent hope and openness to the Spirit would have touched the lives of many others in the course of his ministry at the Temple. For Simeon waiting was joyous and expectant. It would, of course, be wrong to think that all this joy was entirely uninterrupted; there must have been moments over the years when he wondered whether the Messiah would ever come. But as he held the child in his arms he knew that his faithful waiting was over and his joy complete. We too can embrace passionate and active waiting. We are not called, as we wait for the return of Christ, to gaze upward and be of no earthly use. Instead, we need to have a passion for God's kingdom to grow, for justice and peace to fill the earth, for the binding up of the broken hearted and for deep peace to transform a fractured world.

Over the Christian centuries people have popped up from time to time convinced of the imminence of the return of Christ; they have all been wrong. To see the focus of all our hopes it would be better for us to look back to the child in Simeon's arms. There are two different Greek words that translate into the English word 'time'. 'Chronos' means chronological time. I happen to be writing this at 11.15am on a Tuesday morning and will soon be popping downstairs to make a cup of coffee. It's just another day. 'Kairos' is much more about the right time or the opportune moment that lends significance to an event far beyond its place in a series of events that took place on a certain day, week, month, or year. For us that might be our wedding day, the day we heard that we passed our driving test or the day our child or grandchild was born. In the New Testament kairos moments are those at which God says or does something profoundly significant that reveals, fulfils or transforms. When John the Baptist cries, 'The time has come…the kingdom of God is near, Repent and believe the good news!' (Mark 1:15), it is the word kairos that is used. The moment is now, says John, it's time to get off your backsides and do something about it.

As Simeon holds Jesus in his arms we can see that this also is a kairos moment; one that was meant to be. Two people, one at the very end of his life and the other at the very beginning were meant to meet at this precious moment. The text suggests that Simeon wasn't actually on duty when Jesus was brought in to the Temple but that the Spirit gave him a nudge (v 27) to make sure he did not miss the divine appointment. In poetic words that have been known to generations of Anglicans as the 'Nunc Dimittis', sung at evensong week by week, this helpless infant is revealed as the one who has come not just for the people of Israel but the whole world (v 29–32). Simeon, steeped in the traditions of Israel, was able to see a new and further horizon as he gazed at the child who was born for all of humanity.

And then a more sombre note is sounded. Mary has to be prepared for the metaphorical sword that will pierce her soul as a real one is plunged into the side of her son as he dies on the cross. The child's relationship with the people of Israel will be ambivalent and costly. Not everybody was as open to the Holy Spirit as Simeon, not everyone saw the further horizon he could make out. Whilst

Jesus certainly is the Messiah he is not going to lead a war of liberation against the Roman occupiers. He will save, reveal and bring glory but only by walking the way of the cross.

Perhaps it is time for us to become more open to the Holy Spirit. We live in a distracted age and we need to give ourselves time to sit, rest, be open and receive. This cannot be done in a quick couple of seconds in the middle of a busy day. There needs to be intentionality, a definite decision that God will be at the heart of our lives rather than an added extra when we can find a bit of time. Think of Simeon who waited and waited, and then saw. If we follow his example we will find that our hearts and minds will be more open to God's presence and his love. We spend so much time skittering along the surface without ever taking the inner journey to uncover the Christ who lives in the deep places of our hearts where the Holy Spirit is present. As we take that journey it will be, as it was for Simeon, a journey of revelation. It won't always be easy and swords may pierce our souls from time to time. But as we wait on God with expectancy and commitment we might want to spend some time reflecting on the picture before us of Simeon holding the precious child and open our hearts to receive the love revealed at that most wonderful of moments.

Questions: What does 'active waiting' mean to you? Have you ever found your faith growing dim? How can we open ourselves more fully to the Holy Spirit?

Prayer: Lord, give us an openness to the Holy Spirit that we may both wait patiently and work actively for the coming of your kingdom. Amen.

The Samaritan Woman: John 4:1-26
'I who speak to you am he' (v 26)

Many car satellite navigation systems provide a number of alternative ways of getting from A to B including the shortest route, the fastest route and the most eco-friendly route. They also warn of hazards ahead such as roadworks and accidents and route us around them. Because of the entrenched antipathy between Jews and Samaritans, rooted in events of past centuries which had not been forgotten, many Jewish people wishing to travel north to Galilee took a major detour adding considerable time and distance to the journey in order to avoid the hazards of travelling through Samaria (where a racially motivated attack was always a danger).

    Jesus and his disciples took no such detour but had managed to reach the town of Sychar, not a safe place for a group of Jews to be, without incident. The local well is the setting for an encounter that demonstrates just how radical is the Messiah who the Samaritan woman finds sitting by the well she has come to use. In addressing her and asking her for a drink Jesus is effectively driving a coach and horses through time honoured and deeply ingrained prejudices of his time and culture relating to morality, gender and race. To our minds there is nothing particularly unusual in this encounter; but at that time and in that place Jesus' actions were dynamite.

    As Jesus reached across the chasm that separated his people from her people the conversation included the complexities of her own personal life but focused mainly on the offer of living water and the nature of true worship. It's clear that she was someone who found relationships difficult. She has been married five times and presumably divorced five times which would have given her a certain reputation locally (which is why she avoids coming to the well with the rest of the local women in the cooler conditions in the early morning or late evening). Jesus knows all this but starts by asking for her help because he is thirsty; an act in itself culturally scandalous. But it is important in the context of the conversation that Jesus subsequently has with this woman that she has just done something to help him.

As Christians we very properly put a lot of emphasis on what we can do for others both in terms of meeting the needs we see around us and sharing the Christian message. But being able to receive is also important and often undervalued. Back in the early 1990s I was involved in a project that provided finance and resources to help orphan children in the city of Timişoara in Romania not long after the fall of the communist regime. Whilst we were ostensibly there to help it was extremely important that we also allowed people to give to us. We were invited to meals on many occasions and were very much aware that our hosts were giving to us sacrificially; there really wasn't all that much food to go round and a lot of queueing was sometimes required to get it. Yet if we had refused hospitality and effectively said (not necessarily in words but communicated nonetheless), 'we've come here to give to you and you have nothing of value to give to us' it would have reflected an attitude of superiority which, whether we meant it to or not, would have undermined the self-esteem and offended the hospitable nature of those who simply wanted to give something back.

So Jesus talks about water to one who has given him water to satisfy his thirst in the burning heat of the noonday sun; the conversation could not have taken place without his willingness to receive from her. Of course he is talking about a different kind of water and just as Nicodemus, when he hears the phrase 'you must be born again', can only see a ridiculous mental image of people entering their mother's womb a second time (John 3:4), so the Samaritan woman finds it hard to think that Jesus is offering anything other than a supply of drinkable water that will obviate the need to keep visiting the well (v 15). Yet this living or running water is a metaphor for the life and presence of God within the human heart. Jesus is saying that because God is spirit (v 24), worshippers do not have to travel to a specific location to get near to him, whether that be Jerusalem or Mount Gerizim (where the Samaritan Temple stood), instead he longs to find a home in the human heart (John 14:23).

This truth had great relevance for Christians during lockdown as churches were closed and worship moved online. For those without internet access the estrangement from public worship was all the more painful. To know that Jesus lives in our hearts wherever we are and that we can pray, read our Bibles, sing songs of worship and praise and thank him for his love at home or wherever we happen to be has been of paramount importance. However this doesn't mean that going to church is relegated to being an optional extra; the writer to the Hebrews specifically encourages his readers not to neglect the act of worshipping with others (Hebrews 10:25). So, for example, remembering the sacrifice of Jesus as we celebrate Holy Communion together in church is a hugely formative experience for those who follow him, which is why he commands us to do it (Luke 22:19). Yet many clergy also take Holy Communion to members of the church who are housebound, in hospital or in care emphasising that 'place', whilst significant (bearing in mind that Jesus does attach an importance to the Jerusalem Temple in what he says – v 22) is not the be all and end all.

The most important thing about worship, says Jesus, is that it is 'in spirit and in truth' (v 24). When we worship God, whether we are physically in church, watching a service online or reading our Bibles and praying at home, what really matters is that it is a transformative encounter with the living God. We can go to church all our lives and say and sing all the right words but still not have our hearts touched or set on fire. Worship, giving to God what he is worth, is about being open to change; when we find room in our hearts for him it will transform us. The Samaritan woman with the complex love life and terrible reputation locally becomes an evangelist, telling those who shun her in the street and snigger behind her back that she may well have found the Messiah (John 4:29). She isn't sure but the bravery with which she turns to the community that spurned her and opens her heart to them suggests that real transformation has taken place.

She doesn't understand everything and there is still a journey ahead (about which we know nothing). As we worship, not just with our lips but in our hearts and minds in spirit and in truth, we too know that we are only part way there. Worship is more than lip service, it has to be real and reflect a genuine desire to put God at the heart of our lives. Only when we consciously and intentionally place ourselves in the presence of God can the living water flow. We might feel that, having once known that spring within, the water has become somewhat stagnant and we are somewhat becalmed. The Samaritan woman can inspire us to find who we really are once again. If we feel we are walking through a spiritual desert, this passage offers us living water to drink that will well up to eternal life (v 14). It is in drinking deep that the thirst for God that all humans possess, whether they are conscious of it or not, can be satisfied forever.

Questions: What does worship 'in spirit and in truth' mean to you? How can we prevent our Christian lives from becoming dry and running into the sand?

Prayer: Lord Jesus, as we worship you in spirit and in truth, touch our hearts, open us to the streams of living water you offer us, and enable us to share the water of life with others. Amen.

The Paralytic: Mark 2:1-12
'Take your mat and go home' (v 11)

I cannot imagine a world without friends. Our experience of a time when self-isolating and social distancing became part and parcel of daily life made us realise just what a precious gift friendship is. The paralysed man in today's reading was very blessed to have some brilliant mates without whom he would never have met Jesus. Having just arrived back home and no doubt in need of some peace and quiet Jesus is besieged with locals who surround his home meaning that these indefatigable friends have to carry the paralysed man up onto the flat roof of the house in which Jesus was staying, dig through the packed clay and lower him to ground level.

The initial response of Jesus is to the faith of the friends rather than the paralysed man himself yet it is to him that he addresses the words, 'Son, your sins are forgiven', (v 5) that lie at the heart of the story. At that time it was assumed that there was a causal link between sin and suffering yet, in a radical departure from received wisdom, we know that Jesus didn't buy into this (John 9:1-3). Jesus is not saying to the man, 'you've got this condition because you are a particularly bad person', he is simply meeting a fundamental need, shared by every single one of us, for forgiveness.

The legal experts looking on know (rightly!) that only God can forgive sins but fail to recognise the divine authority of Jesus. Exactly what Jesus meant by his self-designation as the 'Son of Man' (v 10) has been debated exhaustively but most obviously is an allusion to a figure described in the book of Daniel (Daniel 7:13-14) who is given authority and is to be worshipped which can only mean he shares the divine nature. What seemed impossible to the teachers of the law was that this authority was being made visible in a residential house in Capernaum that's just had an enormous hole gouged in its roof. But that is exactly what is happening.

What Jesus does by healing the man is make visible a profound depth of love and concern for one vulnerable and sick person that sits alongside the authority he is claiming for himself. The paralysed man himself speaks with actions rather than words in this story; he just gets up, picks up the mat that he is no longer imprisoned on and walks out in a very public demonstration of the authority of Jesus over sin and sickness.

So there were two very significant things that Jesus did for the paralysed man. Firstly, he healed him physically, thereby delivering him from a life of complete dependency and opening new opportunities to him such as being able to work, to be free to go exactly where he wanted, to build new relationships, to marry and have children or even to make a mess of things. Whilst his healing ministry was central to Jesus' vocation and the Christian healing ministry has continued more or less (quite often less) over the centuries, Paul's thorn in the flesh (2 Corinthians 12:7-9) and Timothy's frequent illnesses (1 Timothy 5:23) resonate with our own lived experience that many people of deep Christian faith and commitment are not healed from sicknesses and disabilities. One thing worth throwing in here, of course, is that healthcare provision is now off the scale better than it was in Jesus' day and that there is actually a miraculous element to that which is often overlooked. God is just as much at work (and far more frequently!) through surgeons and other health professionals as he is through those involved in the church's healing ministry. I wonder if God's response to Paul's pleading regarding his 'thorn' helps us to understand why suffering is as much a part of life for Christians as it is for everybody else; 'My grace is sufficient for you, for my power is made perfect in weakness' (2 Corinthians 12:9). So much learning and transformation takes place in the crucible of suffering. I have experienced that as will many reading these words. There are times when we know in our innermost being that, 'when I am weak, then I am strong' (2 Corinthians 12:10).

This, of course, entirely undermines any belief that sickness or disabilities of any kind are judgements of God. The idea of redemptive suffering, as we see in the passion and death of Jesus, allows no place for this kind of thinking (which has nonetheless proved remarkably enduring). Whilst we can sometimes see, for instance in the context of drug and alcohol abuse, that suffering is a consequence (for want of a better term) of harmful behaviours, that does not mean that an illness or disability or any other kind of particular problem any of us struggle with means that we are receiving a specific punishment from God. My experience of pastoral ministry over the years informs me that this is something people do worry about.

A corollary of this is that we are often unable to explain the reasons for specific suffering. There are times when gut wrenching anguish such as that associated with a distressing long-term illness means that the search for any kind of meaning is lost in the pain. The French Catholic poet Paul Claudel wrote that, 'Jesus did not come to explain suffering or remove it. He came to fill it with his presence.' Many of those who knew and loved Jesus similarly found themselves unable to come to terms with his suffering and death. It was only in the light of the empty tomb that a hope that reached into and went beyond suffering became apparent.

The second significant thing Jesus did was to offer the paralysed man the forgiveness of sins, (which is what got him into hot water with the legal experts looking on – v 6–7). It is very clear that, to state the obvious, this man is not alive today which means that at some point in the future he got sick and died. So whereas his physical healing was wonderful, increased his quality of life dramatically and filled him with faith and hope, it was of temporal significance. His experience of forgiveness, however, was eternally significant and reminds us that healing is about more than bodies temporarily being made to work properly again but encompasses our mental, emotional and spiritual lives. Many of us, Christians very much included, carry guilt around with us – I look back even to mistakes made decades ago and still wince every now and again. Sometimes these memories can chain us to the past meaning that we are unable to apprehend the extraordinary beauty of the love that God offers to us today. There is nothing you or I have done or could ever do that would somehow stop God from loving and forgiving us. That doesn't mean that acts of selfishness, cruelty or thoughtlessness don't matter and there are times in life when we will need to face the consequences of our actions. Yet God's love is persistent and addresses us and all of humanity every moment of our lives did we but know it. In receiving God's forgiveness the paralysed man discovered, probably much to his surprise, the deepest truth about himself; that he was loved by God. That is our deepest truth also.

Questions: Do you still feel guilty for things you thought, said or did in the past? Imagine yourself to be face to face with Jesus; what do you think he would say to you?

Prayer: Lord Jesus, thank you for your healing love. Help us to open our hearts and minds to you to receive all that you offer to us and to share it with others. Amen.

The Woman Subject to Bleeding:
Mark 5:24b-34
'Your faith has healed you' (v 34)

In the days when you could just turn up for a football match at the ground of one of the top clubs and pay to go through the turnstiles I went with some friends to Anfield, the home of Liverpool Football Club, to see them play Barcelona in the European Cup (which has since evolved into the cash cow known as the Champions League). In those days the Kop was a standing terrace behind one of the goals and I can vividly remember, whenever the play came down our end, being lifted off my feet in a great wave of people and carried in the air several yards down the terrace before being carried up and back to my starting point when play moved up the other end.

Today's story describes a chaotic crowd of people trying desperately to get close to Jesus at a time when he had quite a reputation as a healer around the towns and villages of Galilee. He is on his way to the house of Jairus, a local synagogue official whose 12-year-old daughter is close to death, when something quite strange happens. When Jesus heals people, it is usually done intentionally and out of love and compassion yet here is an example of an inadvertent healing which Jesus only becomes aware of after the event in that 'power had gone out from him' (v 30). It feels a little impersonal; almost as if Jesus worked on a battery which lost a bit of its charge as its power caused the woman's internal bleeding to cease instantaneously. Perhaps this is one reason why Jesus doesn't allow the woman to scuttle away unnoticed after receiving the healing she desperately craved. As we reflect on this woman who now stands face to face with Jesus let's think about the ramifications of her condition for a moment.

We need to consider firstly what it was doing to her body. She had been 'subject to bleeding' for twelve long years (v 25). Whether this was caused by heavy menstrual bleeding, or some other medical condition isn't clear but whereas in today's NHS she would have been able to visit her local GP and be referred to a consultant if necessary, back then she was in the hands of doctors with very rudimentary knowledge who charged her for the privilege of consultations which only made matters worse (v 26). Her condition was not life threatening, unlike Jairus's daughter she is not dying, but it was both painful and distressing on a daily basis. It meant that she and anything she touched was regarded as ritually unclean (Leviticus 15:25-27) and as a result of this she was excluded from the life of the synagogue of which Jairus, whose daughter she was preventing Jesus from seeing, was an official. The effect of this ritual exclusion was that anybody else coming into contact with anything she had lain on, sat on or even just touched would also become unclean. It's an ancient example of social distancing and the restrictions and lockdowns we experienced during the pandemic give us an idea of the fear that lurked behind these beliefs and practises.

So secondly what was it doing to her mind? As one routinely shunned and excluded she must have led an incredibly lonely life. For many vulnerable people the pandemic meant many months of not being able to see family and friends and they will have had an understanding of what her feelings were. However she did not have access to zoom, social media or a telephone; she was to all intents and purposes alone in the world. If the pandemic taught us one thing it is the value of friendship; we were certainly not made to be alone. Hence the desperation of this woman who puts herself at the heart of something akin to an enormous rugby scrum to get close to Jesus. She is physically healed, something she realises instantly, but she still needs Jesus – he isn't a magician dispensing healings without engaging with the people he comes into contact with. It isn't battery power but God's loving, life giving power that has healed this woman and there needs to be a conversation. That's why Jesus keeps looking; he isn't going to let her slip away.

There are two important things their conversation achieves. Firstly because her healing now becomes public knowledge it makes it much easier for her to be accepted back into the community. Jesus is taking a risk here with his own reputation because according to the letter of the law he himself has been rendered unclean simply by having her touch his garment (even though his disciples make the valid point that in the chaos nobody would have had a clue who had touched his clothes – v 31). But her healing and restoration have to be public; Jesus is not just concerned with her physical healing; he wants to heal the whole person. He wants her to be able to be close to any family she may have, he wants her to be able to go to the synagogue, he wants her to feel valued, wanted and loved.

Secondly it clarifies the role that her faith played in her healing, as Jesus puts it; 'Daughter, your faith has healed you (v 34). It may not have been fully formed, but a desperate kind of hope that touching the healer's cloak might just deliver her was enough. She was only at the beginning of her journey of faith, but she was free. Not just free from the pain and discomfort of her medical condition but from the experience of waking up each day knowing that she would spend that day alone and as an object of fear. We can only imagine what that had been doing to her sense of self-esteem.

We might well feel that our faith is a fragile flower and very much prey to the slings and arrows of outrageous fortune. As we look at other Christians whose faith seems so much stronger and who seem to know so much more about the Bible than we do we can sometimes feel like giving up. Apart from the fact that those we regard in that way almost certainly have issues of their own we can see in this story that even a 'last resort' kind of faith with very little knowledge and understanding but with a deep longing for a different kind of life – whatever that might mean for us in the context of our own lives – evinces a response from Jesus. And the fact that, for us, our engagement with Jesus might or might not result in physical healing, doesn't mean that our faith and walk with Jesus is any the less meaningful and significant. Jesus' wider concern for the mental, emotional and spiritual scars that this unknown woman would have potentially carried with her long after her physical healing is a very significant part of the story.

It is our understanding of how Jesus accepts us with all our doubts, questions, hang-ups, fears and uncertainties that will help us as Christians to offer a non-judgemental welcome to others who come searching even as they are not quite sure what they are looking for. Jesus takes anyone and everyone as they are and where they are and invites them on the journey of faith. Just like Rome, that cannot be built in a day and the Christian life is not a beauty contest in which we are endlessly comparing ourselves to others. We are all broken in one way or another and the acknowledgement of this is an essential prerequisite for growth in spiritual life and faith. As we embark on, continue or re-engage with the life of faith we will always be encountering the love of God who forgives what is past, accepts who we are today and shapes and guides our future. Even in the chaos that sometimes constitutes our daily lives, it's all rather wonderful!

Questions: Have you ever experienced chaos in your spiritual life? How has living through that shaped your walk with Jesus today and how might it shape where you go from here?

Prayer: Lord, accept us as we are and lead and guide us into the future you have prepared for us. Amen.

The One Who Is 'For Us': Mark 9:38-41
'He was not one of us' (v 38)

The 2020 presidential election emphasised the fault lines that now run through society in the United States of America. I read recently of one person cancelling Christmas plans and another moving her wedding date in order to avoid meeting family members on the other side of the increasingly wide political chasm that is causing such damaging division. The political question in an increasing number of countries seems to be, 'are you with us or against us'?

This sort of exclusive mindset has been the cause of some of the deepest wounds of Christian history such as when, in 1054, the Roman Catholic Pope and the Eastern Orthodox Patriarch mutually excommunicated each other causing a tear in the body of Christ that remains unhealed to this day. In 1204, those who had embarked on the Fourth Crusade went even further and destroyed the Christian city of Constantinople, raping nuns and killing indiscriminately as they went about it. To the Crusaders, the people of Constantinople were not 'their kind of Christians', and were therefore fair game. An apology, from Pope John Paul II, in which he stated, 'it is tragic that the assailants, who set out to secure free access for Christians to the Holy Land, turned against their brothers in the faith. The fact that they were Latin Christians fills Catholics with deep regret', took 800 years to arrive.

In today's reading Jesus himself is completely relaxed about the activities of the unnamed exorcist who is worrying John for the simple reason that he is, 'not one of us'. Maybe the stranger had seen Jesus teaching, healing and casting out demons and been inspired to follow suit; we just don't know. Neither do we know anything about his understanding of who Jesus was and what his ministry was all about. We'll assume that it was even more limited than that of the disciples whose own grasp on things was pretty shaky at this stage. Yet Jesus doesn't ask his disciples to grab him and bring him over for a grilling to see what he's about neither does he seem at all interested in finding out more about him or regard him as any kind of threat.

The simple challenge to John is that if this exorcist is performing miracles in Jesus' name how can he be an adversary and why on earth should anybody try to stop him (v 39)? Yet still today Christians are looking at other Christians from different traditions and maintaining that they are not 'one of us'. Within the Christian church there have always been different understandings of key elements of the faith such as the Bible, the Eucharist, the Church, the Mission of God in the world and the scope of salvation. It is very important that the conversations we continue to have about all these issues and many others remain friendly, mutually affirming and generous. All too often, however, they are bitter, spiteful and lacking in any kind of warmth. What so often bedevils the conversations we need so much to keep going is the belief that 'we' (whichever part of the Christian tradition 'we' belong to) are absolutely right in what we believe which means that 'they' are necessarily entirely wrong. This often leads people to look on those who take a different view (which could even be a somewhat nuanced version of what they themselves believe) as not proper Christians at all. Now obviously all Christians believe things about Jesus Christ, his death and resurrection and the way in which his followers should behave in the world today but the misguided belief that you can have this faith thing completely buttoned up betrays a breath-taking arrogance entirely out of sympathy with the generosity of spirit Jesus extends to the unnamed exorcist that John so disparages.

Of course, for Jesus, any belief is meaningless if your actions don't stack up; as he says elsewhere, 'by their fruits, you will recognise them' (Matthew 7:16). It isn't necessarily those who prophesy, drive out demons or even say, 'Lord, Lord' who are getting it right. Rather it is those who demonstrate in the way they live their lives that they are attentive to the will of God (Matthew 7:21-22) who are on a meaningful journey of faith. It is noteworthy that here and elsewhere, as in his dealings with the religious authorities of his day, Jesus reserves his harshest criticism for those who say one thing and do another (Matthew 23:27-28). That is why the final verse of our short passage is so important; anyone who does something as seemingly insignificant as offering a thirsty person a drink of water in Jesus' name is getting it right. The clear implication is that all of us who take the Christian life seriously should be prepared to work, worship and pray alongside those who, like the unknown exorcist for John, are not part of our particular Christian tradition and who may have different understandings, ways of worshipping and doing mission to those we most readily relate to. Which begs the question of how well we know people who attend other churches in our community? So why not go along to a different church than your own from time to time and get to know some of your fellow Christians who do things differently. And do this with an open heart as one seeking to learn and grow rather than taking into that experience a sense of spiritual superiority.

There is an echo in this passage of the Parable of the Sheep and the Goats (Matthew 25:31-46) in which those who minister to Jesus himself by feeding the hungry, giving the thirsty a drink, inviting in the stranger, clothing the naked and visiting the sick and those in prison are entirely unaware of the full significance of what they are doing. In the light of this I'm tempted to push the envelope a bit further and suggest that anyone at all who offers a thirsty person a drink of water or offers any act of kindness to a fellow human being, whatever their beliefs might be (in other words, people of all faiths and none), shares in the compassionate work that is humanity's shared vocation. What Jesus is implying here is that such people, who show themselves by their actions to be doing the work of God, are in an important sense our partners in mission; something implicitly acknowledged by the fact that, as well as Christian relief agencies such as Tear Fund, Christian Aid and CAFOD, the charities who work together on the Disasters Emergency Committee include Islamic Relief and the secular agency Oxfam. This means that when workers from Oxfam dig a bore hole in a village in Africa providing the residents with access to clean water, or when Islamic Relief feed those facing starvation because of the conflict in Yemen, Christians should rejoice because the thirsty are being given a drink and the hungry are being fed.

None of this compromises our own Christian beliefs; after all elsewhere in the Bible Paul quotes Greek philosophers Aratus and Epimenides as part of his presentation of the good news in Athens (Acts 17:28) and the compiler of the book of Proverbs includes a section based on an Egyptian wisdom book called The Instruction of Amenemope (Proverbs 22:17-24:22). The message seems to be that 'even though these people don't believe what we believe, when they are saying and doing good things God is at work'. God is working on a much bigger canvas than is often apparent to us with our limited perspective; something that should both challenge us and make us glad.

Questions: Where can you see, both around you and in your own heart, an 'us and them' mentality? How might you challenge this and be changed yourself in the process?

Prayer: Lord, give us generosity of spirit, an open heart, and the vision to see what you are doing in the world and be part of it. Amen.

The Widow of Nain: Luke 7:11-17
'I say to you, get up' (v 14)

As a curate long ago I remember knocking on the door of a house one particular evening as part of an ongoing visiting project. It was entirely random that I was on that doorstep that night but one member of the family living there, who had no previous connection with church, had just that day finished reading a copy of John's Gospel. It had, in his words, 'changed him' and this 'chance meeting' was an important moment in his spiritual journey as we were able to talk through then and there what he had been reading and its impact on him.

Today's reading is about Jesus and his disciples being in the right place at the right time; a 'chance encounter' as they happen to enter the village of Nain in the middle of a funeral procession involving the entire community. A mother is burying her only son having already, at some time in the past, buried her husband. Not only is it a deeply felt personal loss, it potentially leaves her destitute as the two men who could provide her with an income are now both dead.

Let's just pause a moment and consider the intuitive emotional response of Jesus in this passage. Mark tells us that 'his heart went out to her' (v 13). Jesus encountered tragic and distressing situations throughout his ministry and in spite of (or because of) the fact that he was so often able to provide miraculous healing this would surely have taken its toll on him. Yet as he watches the funeral of an unknown person in a town that wasn't his home his heart is full and he feels for the woman's loss so keenly that he cannot stand by. It is a reminder to us that Jesus is not the kind of miracle worker who rises above it all and is untouched by the pain and sorrow he encounters; there is always a cost to those who really care and there surely was for him. It's no surprise, then, that he very often went off on his own for hours on end, much to the consternation of the baffled disciples

(Mark 1:35-37), to pour it all out to his heavenly Father and ask for ongoing strength for the task.

So it's important that we understand the real emotional engagement that Jesus makes with this bereaved mother. We can perhaps imagine silence falling as he gently encourages the mother to still her tears. Time seems to stand still as he approaches the young man's bier with the intention of significantly delaying his burial. As he touches it there is perhaps a sharp intake of breath as any such contact would, according to the beliefs of the time, render him unclean – once again Jesus goes out on a limb. As life returns to the dead body and words pour forth from his mouth he is 'given back' to his mother (v 15). His life henceforth is a divine gift which will profoundly shape the lives of both mother and son in the years to come.

Two thoughts occur. Firstly that although this mother received her child back and Mary, even after having her soul pierced as she watched her son die naked on a Roman cross, was a witness to his resurrection, all other parents who face the loss of a child do so without the happy ending. I once heard of a priest visiting a family who had lost a child and remarking, 'this isn't God's fault, you know'. I wouldn't have blamed them for ejecting him from the premises without ceremony. Those who have experienced such crushing loss and those who have ministered to them will understand the impossibility of explaining why, for instance, childhood cancers take such young and precious lives. Jesus' ministry was a signpost pointing us to what the kingdom of God looks like; it was never designed to establish a universal panacea for the world's pain or provide us with a way of explaining it. This is why there are times when words do more harm than good; sometimes just being there speaks more eloquently than a thousand words.

Secondly we need to remember that by raising her son, Jesus ministered to this mother on more than one level. We noted earlier that as he turned her tears of mourning to tears of joy he also addressed her financial vulnerability. In a previous study we noted the plight of widows in the days when most women relied entirely on their menfolk for financial security. In the course of Paul's detailed instructions to Timothy he makes it clear that those who fail in their duty to provide adequately for vulnerable family members have 'denied their faith' (1 Timothy 5:4,8). The son will now have the opportunity to fulfil his own responsibilities to his mother.

Visiting the bereaved and the sick, conducting baptisms, weddings and funerals, leading worship and preaching, leading Bible studies and helping people think through their own personal faith and walk with God are a central parts of the church's vocation and in parish ministry I spent lots of time doing all of those things. Yet churches are also involved in running food banks, debt counselling services and breakfast clubs for children from low income families as well as helping people into employment, providing street pastors for city centres at weekends and providing food, drink and accommodation to those living on the streets amongst many, many other things. Christians are also involved in mission and relief projects across the globe. The day before writing this, my wife and I delivered 137 shoeboxes each filled with such things as notebooks, pencils, hats, gloves and small toys that had been donated by many generous people to a Christian organisation based near Preston who will be taking them to children living in extreme poverty in places as diverse as Romania and Sierra Leone as well as those caught up in the conflict in Ukraine. It's just one small expression of Christian concern among very many.

As far as both the ministry of Jesus and his church is concerned there is no distinction between what we might call the spiritual and the social. By way of a chance meeting in Nain Jesus brought both joy and a more certain future to a widow in a single act of compassion. Whilst global news coverage means that we are all keenly aware of the ocean of need in our less than perfect world, which can overwhelm us if we're not careful, it is important that we all do something rather than nothing in response. The following words of the Franciscan priest Richard Rohr in the context of addressing issues of inequality and injustice particularly struck me when I read them the other day, 'I believe that if we can do one or two things wholeheartedly in our life, that is all God expects.' I think there is great wisdom here and it is in the 'wholehearted' nature of whatever we do in response to God's call that the personal commitment and sacrifice lies. So what one or two things could you do?

Questions: Do you have difficult questions to ask God about things that have happened in your own life or those of people you care about? In what way is addressing poverty and inequality part of the mission of the church?

Prayer: Lord Jesus, you gave the widow her son back, open us to your call and help us to share your gifts generously and wholeheartedly. Amen.

Mary and Martha: Luke 10:38-42
'Mary has chosen what is better' (v 42)

I vividly remember an outing with some friends one Sunday afternoon when my children were young. The nearer we got to our destination the more the rain came pouring down and we eventually had to admit defeat. However the parents of one of our party lived quite nearby so plan B was to knock on their front door. We were made to feel enormously welcome and miraculously, as it seemed, food in abundance was placed before us!

Hospitality was, and still is in Middle Eastern culture, a sacred duty. The house that Jesus visits in Bethany belonged to Martha and she would have felt an obligation to provide a welcome and a meal. So we can understand why she gets a little hot under the collar about her sister spending time with Jesus while she is working hard in the kitchen. Households in which one person does all the chores while others do very little to help don't tend to be happy ones!

However there is a bit more to this than meets the eye. In being 'sat at the Lord's feet' (v 39) Mary was both occupying a male space within the house (women lived in the more private rooms, such as the kitchen) whilst also assuming a male persona as, effectively, a trainee rabbi. Paul uses the same expression to describe his own rabbinic training under Gamaliel (Acts 22:3).

This means that a kaleidoscope of thoughts must have been whizzing round in Martha's mind. Everything from 'who on earth does she think she is, we'll never live this scandal down' to 'how many arms does she think I've got!' The result is that she became thoroughly distracted and was unable to embrace the moment. Jesus was not going to be around for all that much longer, Jerusalem and a Roman cross await , and it is Mary who has made the better choice on this particular day (v 42). I suspect that for most of us life pootles along from day to day without the kind of great excitement or drama experienced by Martha and Mary when Jesus came to visit. Yet the message of this passage is that even when life seems uneventful Christians are called to live attentively, sitting at the feet of Jesus with open hearts and minds listening for and to his voice.

Many Christians find a method of reflecting on each day called 'The Examen' very helpful in this regard. It is a way of prayerfully looking back on the day just past and discerning whether God is speaking to us through some of the emotions we have felt, which may include anger, disappointment, love, gratefulness, envy, anxiety or optimism. It also encourages us to reflect on one event that took place that day, which might be a significant conversation, a task performed, a change of plan, something that went wrong, a surprise, an opportunity taken (or missed), a misunderstanding or a new insight gained. Then, whether the day was really good or pretty lousy, we share our thoughts, including what we might have learned, with God. It may be that we will be giving thanks, saying sorry, praying for somebody, offering praise or asking for God's help. It's really about understanding that God weaves his presence through the fabric of our day to day lives and that nothing that happens to us is bereft of meaning. It's clear that on the day of Jesus' visit Mary understood that better.

Martha was distracted because of her worry and anxiety. In today's world there are many distractions which, sometimes in ways that we are barely conscious of, shift the focus of our lives away from the call to sit at Jesus' feet. Many today, (myself included!) need to reflect on the number of times a day we consult our mobile phones and tablets. So, we think, I'll just check emails, WhatsApp messages, the news, Facebook, the weather app, how many steps I've done today and on and on it goes. None of these activities are at all wrong in themselves; it's great that we can, for example, communicate so easily with one another, share photos and videos and check our fitness levels. During the pandemic the internet provided churches with the ability to stream services online and Zoom and other conferencing apps enabled families and friends to keep in touch with one another in ways that would have been impossible a few decades ago. The problem is that not only is it possible for phones, tablets, laptops and computers to gobble up time without us noticing, they can also fill us, along with Martha, with worry and anxiety. It has been well said that going on the internet is the last thing you should do to try and diagnose a medical condition. It reminds me of the opening chapter of Jerome K. Jerome's comic novel Three Men and a Boat in which the narrator, having been looking through a medical encyclopaedia, decides that the only condition he doesn't have is housemaid's knee!

What this kind of distraction can do is shift the focus of our lives away from a securely anchored relationship with God. When we are distracted (by whatever is claiming our attention) it is very often spending time with God that is the casualty. It won't be long before a sense of unreality, that God if he's there at all is a long way away, permeates our being. This is particularly relevant to our use of social media. Facebook and other platforms are not evil in themselves, one Facebook group I belong to is dedicated to old photos of Chester, the city I grew up in, and many of them are fascinating. But it's clear to many now that social media platforms are also being used to manipulate the way people think about important issues by spreading falsehoods such as the allegations of fraud in the 2020 presidential election in the USA which have no basis whatsoever in reality. If we're spending hours and hours on our devices and little or no time with God our spiritual lives must inevitably suffer.

But with Martha, there was a further element to her distraction previously alluded to. Jesus' approval of Mary being a de facto trainee rabbi represents an enormous challenge; according to her and her culture's way of thinking this role was most definitely a male preserve. 'Martha, Martha', says Jesus as he encourages her to grasp that what Mary was doing – listening to him – was the one thing needed at that moment. Being a disciple of Jesus, now as then, involves being open to change in every part of our lives including our beliefs, our lifestyle, our relationships and our values. Change is difficult, especially as we get older, and it is tempting to draw the comfort blanket of familiarity around ourselves whilst looking the other way. Yet we live in a fast moving world that is facing enormous challenges and where change is rapid and accelerating and this will involve new ways of being church, presenting the good news and caring for the planet. It is this need to spend time at the feet of Jesus, learning from him and asking the question 'what would you have me do?' that is the reason why, in Martha's house that day, Mary chose what is better.

Questions: What are things that distract you most and prevent you from spending more time with God? What things do you feel most anxious about and how often do you share your worries with God?

Prayer: Lord, forgive us for being so distracted. Help us to sit at your feet daily and learn more about you that we may better serve you in a changing world. Amen.

The Man Healed of Leprosy: Luke 17:11-19 'Were not all ten cleansed' (v 17)

These days a journey from Samaria to Galilee would entail crossing the wall separating the Palestinian West Bank from Israel, something that many Palestinians are unable to do. For safety reasons pilgrims travelling from Jerusalem to Galilee have to drive east down to Jericho, near to the border with Jordan, and then turn north rather than take a more direct route.

Even back in the time of Jesus it wasn't a safe place; the bitterness and hatred that could be traced all the way back to the division of Israel into two separate kingdoms over nine hundred years previously meant that this border area was a risky place to be travelling (the context for the Parable of the Good Samaritan). The best part of a thousand years is a very long time to be bearing grudges!

There is a clear link in this story to Jesus' earlier parable (Luke 10:25-37) because in both cases the unexpected hero is a Samaritan. In Jesus' parable a member of that community goes to enormous lengths out of a genuine concern for the welfare of a half dead Jewish man who was supposed to be his sworn enemy. In the real world setting of our passage the only one of ten men healed of leprosy who bothers to come back to thank Jesus is a Samaritan. This means we have to consider this passage from two different perspectives.

Firstly and most obviously it is about the need to be thankful. We can imagine all ten of those healed by Jesus being caught up in the excitement of being able to return to their families after months, if not years, of exclusion and isolation. The impact of this on their mental health is reflected in the intensity of their pleas for restoration (v 13). And all ten are healed; their healing is not dependent on their returning to give thanks and leprosy does not flare up again because they went straight home. This healing is an act of unconditional love and, as such, is done freely. The fact that it doesn't seem to have led to spectacular spiritual growth for all but one of the ten might make us doubt their faith. Yet Jesus makes it quite clear that faith played a key role in the healing (v 19), something which must surely have applied equally to the absent nine. Perhaps it was just that in the excitement of the moment and the rush to get home they simply forgot to come back and say thank you. It may even be that some of them regretted their omission later but felt that the moment had passed. Sometimes when you mean to contact a friend you haven't been in touch with for a while or write a thank you note to somebody who has helped you the longer you leave it the harder it becomes to actually do it. 'Do it now or don't do it all' is often the way it goes. Their faith may not have been as great as the Samaritan but even a small amount of faith in Jesus can apparently make a difference, something I personally find greatly comforting.

The point for us here is that true thankfulness always includes a response. In the case of this Samaritan, it meant coming back to Jesus to let him know how much what was done for him was appreciated. Many people who volunteer to work for charitable organisations such as hospices, mental health charities, cancer care centres and churches do so because they themselves received help when they really needed it and want to give something back as a way of saying thank you. There were a number of cases over the years I was involved in running the Alpha Course when people who had done the course subsequently became involved as leaders and helpers. Other people give financially to charities that have helped them in a difficult time which is another important way of saying thank you. The Holy Communion service is sometimes called 'The Eucharist' which derives from the Greek word 'eucharistia' meaning 'thanksgiving'. This means that at the heart of Christian worship is an act of thankfulness for all that Jesus has done for us. Again and again we share bread and wine, tokens of his broken and pierced body, in thankful remembrance of God's gracious and reconciling love. One significant reason Jesus left us this meal was that we would never take for granted the sacrifice that he made for us; each time the drama of the crucifixion is made real for us in bread and wine it is a reminder that it was for us and for all. Then at the end of the service we are sent out to 'live and work to his praise and glory' or to put it another way, to express our thankfulness to God in the way we serve him day by day. It's why James says that without 'works' (which, for him, very much includes caring for those in need) faith is moribund (James 2:14-17, 26).

Secondly we need to consider the implications of the Samaritan being the hero of the story. It's interesting that in calling him a foreigner (v 18) Jesus identifies himself with the Jewish race. He doesn't do this in a narrow nationalistic sense, I think, but to emphasise the omission of the other nine, who we assume to be Jewish, in failing to come back. In affirming the faith of a Samaritan Jesus is breaking new ground. We have to wait until Acts 10, when Peter is shown a vision and sent to the house of Cornelius, a gentile Roman Centurion, to find him and his fellow believers beginning to tumble to the fact that, as he puts it, '…God does not show favouritism…' (Acts 10:34). Convincing his Jewish followers that God wanted to bless Gentiles was always going to be a tough nut for Jesus to crack. Our own age is one in which nationalism, factionalism and populism are once again raising their ugly heads triggering the brutal war Russia has unleashed on Ukraine as well as ongoing conflicts in Nagorno Karabakh, Yemen, Ethiopia, Syria, South Sudan and Myanmar. The suffering this has caused to the many victims who have been killed, maimed, bereaved and forced to leave the communities they have lived in their whole lives is such that we often can't bear to look. Many other regions and individual countries are becoming bitterly divided along ethnic or political grounds – the United Kingdom and the United States of America are two good examples of where this kind of division is on the increase. The message of Jesus Christ is that the human family has a fundamental unity rooted in the fact that Jesus died for all regardless of race or ethnicity. This grateful Samaritan is a signpost pointing us to truths that transcend the divisions that scar our beautiful world reminding us that love, the self-giving love that we see in Jesus, must and will win the day because the risen Christ has triumphed over hate in all its forms and invited us all to be citizens of an eternal kingdom of love, life and peace.

Questions: What do you need to say thank you to God for today? In what ways should living with a thankful heart shape our lives?

Prayer: Lord Jesus, thank you for all that you have done for us. Help us never to take you for granted and to respond in the giving of our lives to your service. Amen.

Zacchaeus: Luke 19:1-10
'Today salvation has come to this house' (v 9)

Zacchaeus was perhaps a bit like the school bully, a person nobody liked but everyone was afraid of. This was first and foremost because he was collecting taxes on behalf of the hated Roman authorities and you had no choice but to pay him if you didn't want to land in hot water. As a chief tax collector he would have staff working under him and would be in an ideal position to cream off whatever he wanted and make himself extremely wealthy; something he took full advantage of. He lined his own pockets at the expense of others and, to cap it all, he was not even a Roman, he was 'a son of Abraham' which made him, in many people's eyes, a collaborator.

And yet, if you will pardon the pun, there was something in his life that didn't add up. He had everything he wanted materially and you would have thought that he would be the last person to show any interest in the itinerant rabbi with his uncompromising views on the perils of wealth. So why is he scrambling up a tree to get a better view? None of those who worked for him or were being cheated by him would have known it, but he was a deeply unhappy man; one of very many who have discovered that possessing everything you could possibly want and more does not bring fulfilment or contentment but is actually a road to nowhere.

This story is about how it is possible, whoever you are and however far down the wrong road you have travelled, to embrace change. I find it inspirational to hear of people who have found themselves in the grip of addiction, whether that be to drink, drugs, gambling, food, computer games or whatever, who manage to turn their lives around and get back on track. I wonder how much of an addiction money had become for Zacchaeus and how much of his life he had spent worshipping at the shrine of mammon? And yet there is still hope for him.

As for the locals, they did not share that hope! It's clear from the text that Jesus' decision not just to talk to Zacchaeus but to go to his house for a meal did not go down well at all (v 7). Their unanimous assessment was that he was the last person whose hospitality Jesus should be enjoying, especially considering the possibility that the food they would eat was paid for with fraudulently obtained funds. They may well have subscribed to the cynical but very often accurate view that people like Zacchaeus are incapable of taking their noses out of the trough long enough to even notice the pain and hardship they are causing.

But Jesus was able to see not just what Zacchaeus was (corrupt and deeply unpopular) but also what he might become. His world was one where anything is possible and where nobody is beyond redemption. We're not given any details about the meal Zacchaeus and Jesus shared; without doubt they talked about many things. But by the end Jesus was listening to a changed man who had a completely different purpose in life. After a transformative tea Zacchaeus committed to giving 50% of his dishonest gains away and repaying fourfold anyone he had cheated (I'm sure they very quickly formed a queue). In promising to do this he went way beyond the Law of Moses which stated that the amount defrauded plus 20% should be repaid (v 8 see Numbers 5:7). It's interesting that Jesus accepts Zacchaeus' offer of restitution and does not insist, as he did in the case of the Rich Ruler in the previous chapter, that he give away every single last penny (Luke 18:22). Maybe it was the fact that Zacchaeus himself offered to give such a large sum of money away off his own bat (as far as we can tell) that made a difference.

The upshot of all this is that somebody who had lost his vocation as a son of Abraham has been found and saved; the Good Shepherd has found one of his lost sheep and brought him home. In doing so he upset many of the citizens of Jericho and would have become ritually unclean in the eyes of many by sharing food and drink with a collaborator. Yet his core task was to reach out to all those blundering around in a darkness often of their own making and lead them into the light. That is still a core task for today's church which means reaching out to the kind of people many people would rather not associate with. That is why prisons have chaplaincy teams offering pastoral care and a listening ear to people who, for whatever reason, have made a mess of their lives by committing criminal acts. This expresses eloquently one of the central truths of the Christian faith; that God doesn't give up on anybody and ceaselessly reaches out in love to everybody. This doesn't mean that God condones criminal, addictive, abusive, narcissistic or destructive behaviour – very far from it. It was because evil has disfigured the world and can't just be waved away with a flick of the divine hand that God gave his only Son in an act of painful and generous love. The Bible makes it abundantly clear just how seriously God takes the fact that we have all lost our way.

Which people assume, or have assumed, the role of Zacchaeus in our lives? They might be people we know or have known who we feel we have been hard done by, who have upset us in a way that we have found impossible to forgive, who get on our nerves, who we have written off as a bad job or who have done well out of behaving badly. I have sometimes found that when I think about somebody in that way it helps very much to pray for them. If I bring that person into God's presence and ask for his blessing on them (rather than just saying 'please make them easier to deal with!') then I begin to see them more from God's point of view rather than my own more jaundiced perspective. They may be lost in one way or another but God is reaching out to bring them home and the story of Zacchaeus underlines both the possibility of change and the indefatigable nature of God's search for all who are lost.

The bottom line is that all of us are lost in one way or another and we need to remember that there may well be people who find us difficult! The message of the story of Zacchaeus applies to us as well; God is searching for us and every moment reaching out to us in mercy and love did we but know it. All of us have experienced times when it has felt like we were wandering around in the fog unable to see where we are going; when we felt, in one way or another, that we were pretty much lost. The message of the story of Zacchaeus is that all those who are lost are being sought after ceaselessly. It is the amazing grace of God, undeserved but freely offered, that reaches out to us and brings us home.

Questions: Has there been anyone in your life who has been unfair to you, upset you or made you angry? Have you ever tried praying for them?

Prayer: Lord, thank you that you came to find the lost and bring them home. When we are lost, find us and when we encounter the lost give us your compassionate love. Amen.

The Woman Caught in Adultery: John 8:1-11 'Go now and leave your life of sin' (v 11)

The tabloid press are ever looking for sensational headlines – anything that will sell newspapers. I suspect that many of those who write for such newspapers would not particularly like some of their own faults and foibles to be made public. On the other hand good investigative journalism has a hugely important role in uncovering corrupt and criminal behaviour by those who wield power. The risk for anyone judging others is that they run the risk, as equally flawed human beings, of judging themselves (Matthew 7:1-2) – which is what this passage is all about.

The woman caught in adultery was deliberately brought to Jesus in a very public place right in the middle of the Feast of Tabernacles when Jerusalem and its Temple would have been packed with pilgrims. For her it was humiliating and terrifying, like finding yourself on the front page of the tabloids as well as staring a particularly horrible way to die in the face; only the stone that would finally suck the life from her body would end the agony that was coming her way. Yet given that it takes two to tango, where was the other participant in this adulterous fling? The man she was caught with has got away with it even though the Jewish Law was unequivocal in demanding that he too suffer the ultimate penalty (Leviticus 20:10). It is a sad truth that, without in any way condoning her behaviour, her presence and the absence of her lover is typical of the kind of prejudice women have been familiar with since time immemorial. She, rather than he, is the one being used as a pawn in a cynical game of entrapment intended to catch Jesus out in order to arrest him. The religious teachers demand the ultimate penalty for *her* whilst appearing entirely uninterested in where *he* is.

So the trap is set; if Jesus says 'don't kill her' he will be publicly driving a coach and horses through the Law of Moses, but if he says 'go ahead', he will be driving another coach and horses through everything that he has been teaching. Jesus' response is to write on the ground. Tantalisingly we have no idea at all what he was writing but the fact that he continues to do this after his challenge to any of the accusers who are without sin to be the first to hurl a stone suggests that it was to give people, including himself, time to think. Once the elders begin to melt away everyone else takes their cue until Jesus is left alone with the woman.

It's important to see that Jesus does not condone her adulterous behaviour; it isn't the case that he is somehow on her side of the argument and lets her off. But he doesn't condemn her either. Her other accusers all trudged off because they were made to realise that when you live in a glass house you really shouldn't be throwing stones. But Jesus, the one whose sinless life does potentially give him the right to condemn her, refuses to do so. Instead he offers her an opportunity to transform her life and make a new start.

It is Jesus' clear understanding that judgement is meant to be restorative rather than retributive that I think undergirds his words and actions in this story. One wouldn't be forgiven for thinking that quite a lot of judgement in the Old Testament looks pretty vindictive, the Genesis flood and the wholesale slaughter of Canaanite communities by the invading Israelites being cases in point. But the Jewish people returning from exile in Babylon came to understand that God's judgement on them and their consequent journey into exile wasn't a capricious act of revenge because they had turned their backs on him but a 'last resort' attempt to restore and renew their vocation as the people of God (Isaiah 48:17-20). In our passage Jesus is giving us an example of restorative judgement, in effect saying to her, 'whatever you have done wrong, learn from it and move on to better things.' It goes without saying that this would be impossible if she were to end up lying lifeless in the dust.

Judgement is, of course, a key theme in the Bible. Yet there is also a vision of universal restoration present in the earliest Christian proclamation (Acts 3:21) as well as the teachings of Paul (Romans 8:19-21). Add to that Paul's belief that God's intention is that every human being should come to know and embrace the truth (1 Timothy 2:4) and the restorative rather than retributive nature of God's judgement starts to come into focus. We have to do some thinking about what kind of God we believe in. Is he essentially vengeful, dishing out nasty stuff to those who have offended him even to the extent that exclusion from his light and love is permanent and non-negotiable no matter what the torment involved?

Of course we have to take seriously the concept of God as judge. One of the tenets of the Christian faith is that what kind of person you are, how you treat other people and what you believe to be true all matter very much. This means that thoughts, words and actions which are cruel, selfish, hurtful, inconsiderate and hateful, or to put it another way 'sinful', can't just be swept under the table as if they were nothing. Yet as we weigh Jesus' words that he came into the world to save it rather than to judge it (John 12:47) we need to remember that Christianity is, at its heart, a faith that rests on love rather than fear. This in turn rests on the fact that although God judges, he does so mercifully, so much so that he gifts his only Son to atone for human sin in a way that is so vast and mysterious that however we describe it falls far short of its full wonder. Which means, taking us back to the woman caught in adultery, that God does not stand with the stone throwers whose idea of judgement is to destroy, but instead wants her, as the Book of Common Prayer puts it, to 'turn from her wickedness and live'. This means living life in all its fullness as a restored and loving human being.

So when you are tempted, with the tabloid press, to throw metaphorical stones at those who fail to come up to scratch just bear in mind that Jesus gave his life for your sins as well as theirs and that all any of us can do as we kneel at the foot of the cross is to say, 'Lord Jesus Christ, have mercy on me, a sinner.'

Questions: Why do you think people have sometimes found Christians judgemental? How do we reconcile the judgement of God and the mercy of God?

Prayer: Lord Jesus, when we are tempted to judge, remind us of the loving mercy you have shown to us and to all people. Amen.

The Centurion: Matthew 8:5-13
'Go! It will be done just as you believed it would' (v 13)

In the main entrance of the Grosvenor Museum in Chester there is a life size model of a Roman centurion wielding his sword and looking more than ready for battle. Centurions were hardened veterans responsible for training soldiers, maintaining discipline and displaying bravery and resolution on the battlefield. They had 80 men under their command and generally displayed little subtlety when it came to the aforementioned methods of training, disciplining and fighting.

Whilst the centurion in our passage may well have been serving under King Herod Antipas, Rome's client king in the province of Judaea, whose forces were organised in line with the Roman army, he was definitely a gentile (Jews were exempt from conscription) and represented, if at one remove, the might and power of Rome. This man was not a centurion because of who he knew or where he came from; he had been promoted because he had proved himself to be an effective soldier. Or to put it another way, he was good at killing people.

He is, then, a rather improbable character to be waylaying Jesus as he enters the town of Capernaum with an urgent plea on behalf of his ailing servant. Being in actual fact a slave, the servant would normally have been regarded as part of his property with any concept of human rights unknown. The overwhelming majority of people in the centurion's situation wouldn't have cared whether the slave lived or died except for the inconvenience of having to buy another one. The world of the centurion was one of commanding and obeying without question and he himself was one cog in a chain of command which ultimately went all the way up to the Emperor of Rome. Just as he has to do exactly what he is told so those he commands must do the same. There was no room for sentiment of any kind – when you tell somebody to go, come or do this, they unhesitatingly obey (v 9b). If you were serving under the centurion in the heat of battle and he commanded you to mount an attack in which you were likely to be killed you had no choice but to do what you were told.

Yet Jesus says that this battle scarred veteran displays deeper faith than he has yet seen in Israel. What an extraordinary statement! Not only does he display a very particular concern for someone who he regarded as a person rather a piece of property but he also believes in Jesus' ability to heal him. What this says to me is that in spite of the brutalising effects of commanding men who kill and get killed the centurion had not lost touch with his own humanity.

In today's world both war and slavery continue to dehumanise many. It is not just those who fire bullets and drop bombs (often by pressing a button in a military complex thousands of miles away from the conflict zone) causing death and terrible injury but those whose homes and communities are devastated and whose loved ones are killed or maimed who face an all-out attack on their humanity. Modern slavery takes many forms such as human trafficking, forced labour, sexual slavery, child slavery, forced marriage and domestic slavery. Enslavement has not gone away and continues to dehumanise both its victims and its perpetrators.

This comes uncomfortably close to home when we consider firstly that because of our long history of selling arms to Saudi Arabia, many of those who are suffering in the conflict in Yemen are being targeted by weapons made in the United Kingdom and secondly that modern slavery pervades society to a disturbing extent with child trafficking a growing problem in every part of the country.

One of the reasons the centurion retains his humanity and can open his heart to Jesus is that he loves the people he is supposed to feel nothing for. In Luke's version of this story he adds the detail that local leaders come to Jesus pleading the worthiness of centurion's cause because, 'he loves our nation and has built our synagogue' (Luke 7:5). Perhaps the real evidence of his faith is that he is able to see over the cultural, ethnic and religious barriers of his time and understand that people living, working and worshipping on the other side of those dividing lines are as important as anyone else.

Jesus uses harsh words for those who wish to restrict the love of God because it is not just those who consider themselves children of promise who will be at the feast. Jesus' assertion that there will be outsiders present was certainly controversial and yet as the story ends with the healing of the centurion's servant, we see an indiscriminate outpouring of divine love in perfect harmony with his vision.

One key aspect of Jesus' ministry was that he was able to make people who had been dehumanised feel fully human again. Those he healed of leprosy, for example, were not just restored to health but also to the circle of their families and friends ending for some of them long years of rejection and isolation. For the centurion, the local Judaean people were outsiders, he was not there to make friends but to enforce Roman rule. However he had managed to form a relationship with them that was not that of oppressor and oppressed but based on a shared humanity. It is when we think of people as outsiders for whatever reason that we dehumanise them. At the same time, of course, we dehumanise ourselves. God is an inclusive God and asks us to make that real in our daily lives and the lives of our churches.

It might be as simple as the outsider being somebody we don't know. When I was fifteen I started attending a church youth group. Although my elder brothers had previously been members I knew very few people in what was a large group of young people and felt very much on the outside of things. However somebody called Andrew took me under his wing over a number of weeks. He had his own group of friends but would come over to me and chat, suggest a game of table tennis and basically check that I was ok. As time went by I found my feet, my own group of friends and a living faith in Jesus. I cannot even recall Andrew's surname and have not met him for the best part of fifty years and yet he did three things for me. He made me feel welcome, affirmed me as a human being and helped me to find faith; I cannot thank him enough.

It's given me a particular sensitivity to the after church coffee time on a Sunday morning. If somebody is left standing on their own while members of the church chat away in their friendship groups that person will, very justifiably, feel like an outsider – a horrible feeling. The centurion went out of his way to understand and build relationships with those who were outsiders (and to whom he was very much an outsider). Likewise there are times (Sunday morning coffee being one of them) when we will need to go out of our way to include and welcome somebody new who may have come to church with a specific need. It's the kind of thing Jesus did both in this passage and throughout his ministry.

Questions: How might an understanding of God's love as unconditional impact our understanding of the 'good news' of Jesus? How can we live that out?

Prayer: Lord, help us to reach out to those who, for any reason, are outsiders and to offer them a welcome in your name. Amen.

The Canaanite Woman: Matthew 15:21-28 'Woman, you have great faith!' (v 28) (Passion Sunday)

On Passion Sunday we ponder the pain and suffering that Jesus endured on his journey to the cross. Reflecting on how he overcame the deep human aversion to pain as he pleaded to be released from and subsequently accepted the way of suffering and death (Matthew 26:36-44) reveals much about the love he personified.

In the light of that, what on earth is going on in today's passage? Jesus and his disciples are way up north beyond the territory of Israel when they encounter a local woman in desperate need. But it looks like at best Jesus is in no hurry to heal her daughter and at worst has no intention of helping her at all. He responds to her initial cry with silence and then moves on to inform her that she is outside the scope of his mission and uses a racial slur against her (v 26). As Jesus does eventually release her daughter from the evil that has imprisoned her we could, at first reading, understand this encounter as a steep learning curve for him. In the end, in spite of his misgivings, he recognises her faith and responds and in doing so begins to understand that his ministry might have wider ramifications than he had realised up to this point.

The problem with this reading is that, as we saw in the previous reflection, Jesus had already healed the servant of a Roman Centurion (Matthew 8:5-13) and if we cross check with Luke's Gospel we will find that, right from the outset, he was risking his life to make the point that he had not come just to save Israel (using the widow at Zarephath and Namaan the Syrian as test cases). It nearly got him killed before he'd even got started (Luke 4:24-30).

It may well be that, by a process of elimination, the people who really needed to get shaken out of their racial presuppositions were his disciples. It's almost as if he deliberately gives voice to the sullen silence, exclusivist thinking and racial slurs that are present in their hearts (and given voice by their request to Jesus to get rid of her) in order to demonstrate how unacceptable they really are.

What Jesus is doing here is shoving this woman's faith under the noses of the disciples as if to say, 'what do you make of that?!' It is not the only example of shock therapy in the Gospels; his declared intention to go to his death in Jerusalem and his request to wash the feet of his disciples spring readily to mind. What seems to be happening here is that Jesus is demonstrating that real faith, the kind of faith that isn't put off by silence, exclusion or racial slurs, is to be found beyond the boundaries of Israel and in people other than those who self-identify as God's chosen people. Lost sheep can through faith be found, loved, helped and healed in Tyre and Sidon just as much as in Galilee or Jerusalem.

Once the disciples have encouraged Jesus to send this troublesome woman packing we don't hear another word from them. They stand silent as this Canaanite woman, who for them was certainly a 'dog' and who represented a society that had a long history of enmity with the people of Israel, gives voice to a deeper faith than they themselves can muster. I wonder what they are thinking.

Prejudices don't have to be at the surface to be real. Those who give voice to bigotry by going on marches or committing hate crime are not the only ones who feel that way, it's just very often kept under wraps. Prejudice is present when we fail to accept people for who they are as individuals but judge them according to their race, class, age, sexuality, disability or any other category. A key tenet of Christian belief is an unequivocal belief that every human life is sacred because what we all have in common and binds us together as a human family is that we are made in the image of God.

This means that all those who have left their homes and communities to escape war or poverty, those of all races, ethnicities and sexualities, those with disabilities and those of all ages are family. The effect of what the disciples witnessed as Jesus appears to send this outsider back where she came from and then turns everything they have always known to be true on its head by applauding her faith and healing her daughter would have been thought provoking, to say the very least.

We must be aware that similar prejudices and assumptions about people lie deep within our own culture and its morally ambivalent past. An ancestor of mine who was a barrister at Lincoln's Inn for many years spent the last nine years of his life as a senior legal officer in British India, still run at that time (the early nineteenth century) by the East India Company. He was a knight of the realm and, especially as he is not at all typical of my family history, which is mostly peopled by people such as agricultural labourers and bricklayers, it has been interesting to research his life. However my severe doubts about his role as an instrument of empire came to a head when a speech he made following the Third Anglo-Maratha War of 1817–18 which decisively cemented and expanded British rule in India was brought to my attention. The speech, which was to propose a motion congratulating the Governor General on his military success, reflected an unquestioned belief in the superiority of the British race and a consequent justification of a war in which many thousands of Indians were killed.

It was the inability to question his assumptions concerning racial superiority and his support for military action against people who had not asked the British to be in India in the first place which was most shocking to me. There are uncomfortable questions we all have to ask ourselves about inherited assumptions we might have failed to question and consequent prejudices lurking unacknowledged within. It is also something that churches need to address. The inclusive nature of the good news of Jesus Christ is exactly why Jesus' disciples, standing in awed and uncomfortable silence in front of a foreign woman who had just demonstrated that her faith was more inclusive than theirs, needed to be confronted and challenged.

So if we believe that God sent Jesus to die because he wants everybody to be included, there will be practical implications for the life of the church. For instance we will need to raise awkward questions, as touched on with regard to Mephibosheth, about to what extent people with disabilities are able to fully (with the emphasis firmly on the word *fully*) participate in the life of the church including all leadership roles. In my time in ministry a growing awareness of this issue led to action being taken to introduce such things as induction loops, large print service booklets and ramps enabling people with disabilities to access all areas (bearing in mind that the need to be able to climb steps to, for instance, celebrate or help distribute Holy Communion is exclusory). A fully open and inclusive Christian community is a thing of great beauty. It will reflect the passion of Christ and embody his vision of a kingdom open to the poor, the prisoners, the blind and the oppressed (Luke 4:18). The task for the church today is to live out the fundamental truth that God wants everybody to be included. That's as much a challenge for God's people today as it was for the disciples during their trip up north.

Questions: What contemporary attitudes do we see in the reaction of the disciples to the Canaanite woman? How might we address them within ourselves and more widely in the church and in society?

Prayer: Lord, thank you for enduring suffering for us and for all. Help us to reflect your passionate love in all we think, say and do. Amen.

The Little Children: Mark 10:13-16
'The kingdom of God belongs to such as these' (v 14)

It may seem that Jesus' disciples are having a bit of a hard time. Up in Tyre and Sidon they had their cages well and truly rattled and here, as they try unsuccessfully to control access to Jesus, all they get is a telling off. Bringing children to a rabbi for a blessing was not an unusual custom and it's difficult to know what exactly the disciples were worried about. Perhaps it had been a very long day! Not only does Jesus actively want the company of these children (and we can perhaps imagine an excited group of parents pushing their children forward for a blessing), he has a point to make about the way things work in his kingdom – everybody, whoever they are, comes into the kingdom in a childlike (as opposed to childish) way.

We need to remember here that as well as being the Son of God, Jesus was a human being and there must have been a sense of loss in knowing that he would never have children of his own. There are, of course conspiracy theories about him marrying Mary Magdalene, but although it would have been perfectly proper for him to have married (it isn't a sin, after all!) and have children I suspect that once he came to understand his vocation and the suffering that would be entailed he would not have wanted to put a wife and children through the associated trauma. I wonder, though, whether when he spent time in the company of children, he felt a slightly wistful sense that he would never have any of his own. It is a reminder to us that, well before he arrived at the cross, he had already made many sacrifices.

I have read and spoken about this passage many times at services of infant baptism when new members are welcomed symbolically into the family of the church. There is a powerful sense of acceptance and affirmation behind the picture this passage presents to us (v 16). Yet the reason Mark has included it is that children have something very important to communicate to the rest of us about the nature of the kingdom of God and how it is to be received. So what does Jesus mean when he says that we must become 'like a little child' in order to receive the kingdom? To grasp this we need to distinguish between being childish and childlike. Let's go back a little earlier in Mark 9 to where the disciples were embroiled in an argument amongst themselves about which one of them is top dog (Mark 9:33-37). When challenged by Jesus about the nature of the quarrel they can only respond with an embarrassed silence. Their squabble and their silence amply demonstrate the ability of grown men to act in an infantile manner. Responding childishly to the kingdom means wanting to be more important than other people, believing that our understanding of the truth is the only valid one, expecting instant answers to every prayer, getting steamed up when we don't get our own way and regarding those who disagree with us as troublesome nuisances. This approach to faith can and does harm people's faith, split churches and cause heartache to those on the receiving end.

What Jesus does is place a child before the disciples. Children at that time had no rights, as such, and were not considered Roman citizens even if both their parents were. If we glance for a moment at the equivalent passage in Matthew it becomes clear that Jesus is teaching his disciples a lesson about humility (Matthew 18:4), the key attribute of a childlike faith. So if we return to our passage, when Jesus says to his disciples that the kingdom has to be received like a child (v 15) it means there is no room for the power plays they had been indulging in. Receiving the kingdom in a childlike way means thinking of others as being better than ourselves, being open to different understandings of Christian life and faith, persevering in prayer patiently, not insisting that we get our own way (Philippians 2:4) and being gracious towards those who don't see things as we see them.

One key element in receiving the kingdom like a child is the ability to ask questions, it's what children do all the time and how they learn and come to maturity. But being open to new truths and understandings, even if that means letting go of something we have believed for many years, is part of the lifelong learning curve that is an integral part of our Christian journey. People who think that their understanding of, for example, the nature of Christ's sacrifice on the cross or the person and work of the Holy Spirit, is the only game in town and that nobody else has anything to bring to the table are not generally attractive people to be with. There will, of course, always be people attracted to the unquestioned certainty of such an approach. The problem is that this kind of approach will put many others off for life.

A humble faith recognises that we are all childlike in our understanding of the nature of God and what he has gifted us in Jesus Christ. I find myself sometimes, when considering the size and complexity of creation, admitting to myself that in actuality God is way, way, way beyond my ability to understand or even conceive of. When we speak of God as 'Father' that is no more than a metaphor to try and grasp how our relationship with God works. That's fine as long as we understand that God is not male (bearing in mind that there are maternal images of God in the Bible, Hosea 11:3-4; Isaiah 66:13 and Matthew 23:37 are just a few) and exists beyond categorisation. I find myself then looking back at myself and realising how small and insignificant I and every other member of the human family actually is. What empires we try to build when we are here for no more than a brief moment (Psalm 144:3-4).

However Jesus is talking to his disciples and us in our passage today about approaching God with humility, conscious of our own limitations, failings and seeming insignificance, and thereby discovering more of his love for every human being and, indeed, the whole created order. It is precisely here, as we come close to God, that we discern the sacred nature of each of the children that Jesus blessed and indeed of every human life. We only find out who we really are when we uncover the love of God present in the deep places of our hearts silently yet powerfully drawing us into a relationship that, as Paul so memorably affirms (Romans 8:38-39) is unbreakable in time and eternity.

Questions: What do you think it means for us to enter the kingdom like a child? In what ways does asking questions about our faith help us to grow as Christians?

Prayer: Lord, help us to receive you humbly and to know that there is always more to learn. Amen.

Stephen: Acts 6:1-15; 7:54-8: 1a 'And Saul was there, giving approval' (8:1a)

I remember once hearing the vicar of a very busy parish speak about the liberation he felt when a parish administrator was appointed to take some of the load of running the parish from his shoulders. This didn't mean, of course, that what the new administrator would be doing was the less important stuff; administration is one of the spiritual gifts that Paul lists (1 Corinthians 12:28) and things fall apart very quickly if it isn't done properly and efficiently. But it meant that he could focus more effectively and less exhaustingly on his deeply felt calling to mission and pastoral care.

The Apostles had a similar problem to the busy priest; they simply had too much to do. As the number of believers increased so the organisational challenges multiplied. They found themselves being dragged into a quarrel between Aramaic and Greek speaking Jewish Christians concerning the fairness or otherwise of what today would be called a food bank that they were overseeing. We don't know whether the perception among the Greek speakers that the Aramaic speakers were getting preferential treatment was justified or a figment of their imagination. Even if they did have a point the Apostles were certainly not intentionally doing anybody out of their fair share. If anything the church was a victim of its own success; it was growing fast and the leadership structures that had been put in place (which meant effectively that everything got referred to the Apostles) weren't coping with the influx of new believers meaning that something needed to give.

Enter Stephen. The job of sorting out the distribution of food is delegated to a group of seven people, led by him and recognised as being 'full of the Spirit and wisdom' (6:3). The fact that this sharing was known as a 'diakonia', meaning 'service', has led to Stephen and his colleagues being thought of as the first deacons. So whilst this may have been an organisational role it still needed faithful servants who would do it prayerfully and pastorally if the quarrel were to be resolved. Conflict in churches happens more often than it should and sometimes it isn't so much a question of how to avoid it as how best to deal with it when it comes along. Sometimes the disagreements can be fairly mundane in nature; one church council I was a member of had a tough job choosing the colour of the new service books! However when it comes to issues such as the balance between old hymns and new worship songs in Sunday worship or major changes to the pattern of services feelings can run very high. In such circumstances people 'full of the Spirit and wisdom' are worth their weight in gold.

It appears that Stephen and his colleagues were very good at conflict resolution; the problem was quickly sorted out with the result that the church experienced rapid growth. A united church is one that people will want to join! However, as Stephen's ministry grew and developed and miracles became associated with his evangelistic endeavours, he runs into a much more deadly conflict, this time with members of the synagogue. He was a persuasive speaker and when his opponents couldn't best him in debate, they resorted to having him arrested. Christians are called to avoid conflict if it is at all possible but not at all costs. Paul's words to the church in Rome advising that, 'If it is possible, as far as it depends on you, live at peace with everyone' (Romans 12:18) make it clear that Christians should not go looking for trouble but implicitly acknowledge that being faithful to Christ might mean that trouble will find them.

So it is that the martyrdom of Stephen has been shared over the centuries by a very large number of Christians. It was shared by a considerable number of believers because of the edict issued by the Roman emperor Decius in January 250 to the effect that everybody in the empire was required to make a sacrifice to the ancestral gods after which they would be given a certificate (called a 'libellus') to confirm that they had done it. Perhaps we can reflect here for a moment and imagine ourselves in a situation in which we can only avoid conflict and potentially a painful death by denying our Christian faith. I would hope to have the strength to endure, as many believers at that time did at the cost of their lives (there were others who made the sacrifice to save their lives – and that of their families – which created a pastoral problem when they wanted to rejoin the church after the persecution was over). It is however a challenging and uncomfortable thought; especially when we consider that in our own day

Christians in North Korea are given a one-way ticket to a brutal concentration camp along with their families (in an example of guilt by association) if they are identified as believers.

All this should make us grateful for the freedom we enjoy in this country to live out our faith freely even as we offer, as we must, our love, prayers and support to the substantial community of persecuted Christians. It should also make us think twice when we are in danger of getting involved in the kind of conflict Stephen had to sort out at church. The thought of what so many Christians are suffering in North Korea and elsewhere as I write these words and you read them puts the fact that we didn't like some of the hymns or the taste of the after-service coffee when we last went to church into perspective. In fact, our experience of suspending public worship as a result of the pandemic should in itself be a reminder of how precious it is to meet together with our fellow Christians every Sunday even if not everything that is said or done is exactly what we like (which it never can be, of course).

One further thought. The word martyr actually means witness. As Stephen died in a volley of stones, witnessing to his faith in Christ, a young man was watching while he looked after the coats of the stone throwers and cheered them on in his heart (7:58; 8:1a). However, after the event, this young man, better known to us as the apostle Paul, did an awful lot of thinking which came to a head when he met the risen Lord on the road to Damascus. The enormous impact of Paul's journeys and writings on the life of the Christian church means that Stephen's witness and his willingness to die for his faith were not in vain but bore much fruit. So let's be inspired by the sacrifice of Stephen to do what he did and work for peace and unity in the church and the world. Two days before the time of writing a rally organised by Christians and addressed by a number of church leaders led directly to the United States Capitol being stormed violently and five people being killed. Apart from any other consideration (and there are many) it was a terrible witness to the Christian faith.

We are all called, imperfect as we are, to witness to the peace and love of Jesus as with patience, forbearance and generosity of spirit, we share the precious truths that have been entrusted to us.

Questions: What are the consequences of conflict within the church? How do we, as Paul puts it, 'live at peace with everyone?'

Prayer: Lord, you have called your church to be one in heart and mind. Help us to love one another, be patient with one another and suffer with one another as we witness to your grace and truth. Amen.

Tabitha: Acts 9:36-43
'Tabitha, get up!' (v 40)

Most human beings who have populated planet Earth over the millennia have left no historical record of their presence; they have lived and died in complete obscurity. But for her encounter with Peter, Tabitha would have been one of them. She was just an ordinary person living in an ordinary house in an ordinary town and yet her example of Christian service is one that all of us should take to heart.

Luke introduces her to us as a disciple. The Greek word *mathetria,* meaning disciple, is given its feminine form reminding us straight away that the designation isn't restricted to the twelve men who were Jesus' closest associates. In the biblical sense of the word a disciple is anyone who follows Jesus, learns from his teachings, and tries to live them out. Tabitha seems to have taken her discipleship very seriously, was extremely generous with her time and resources and was undoubtedly greatly loved by all who knew her.

That would explain why, when she died, her fellow disciples ran to fetch Peter, who happily just happened to be in the vicinity. At this point in the story Peter is on the cusp of a very important discovery. After his ministry to Tabitha, a game changing rooftop vision finally gets it into his thick head (I'm not having a go at him, I have one of those too) that the good news is not just for Jews but for everyone (Acts 10:9-16; 34-35). So even though he is an apostle and the agent through whom an amazing miracle takes place, he has not stopped being one of Tabitha's fellow disciples. It is a reminder to us that the lifelong learning curve intrinsic to the discipleship journey does sometimes include unlearning things we thought we knew.

Tabitha's discipleship journey had a specific focus on caring for the poor for whom she has been tireless in making and supplying clothes. The fact that Peter, upon entering Tabitha's room, is surrounded by a group of widows eagerly thrusting items of clothing she had made for them in his face reflects both the vulnerability of such women at that time and the depth of their gratefulness to her. She seems to have gone about her very practical ministry without a great deal of fuss; one imagines that she simply got on with it using the God given talents she possessed.

When, through Peter's Spirit inspired ministry Tabitha was raised from death, it enabled her (we presume) to continue her ministry but also acted as a catalyst for the spread of the good news in the area (v 42); there's nothing like a miracle to get people talking. However having been brought out of obscurity momentarily as a result of an apostle's visit, Tabitha immediately falls out of the limelight and continues her work under the radar.

I know many people like Tabitha who quietly go about the business of caring for others. They don't want a reward or their names up in lights; they just want to get on with it. I have a link, alluded to earlier, with a local Christian charity project which procures and fills cardboard shoeboxes with items, such as combs, toothbrushes and toothpaste, toys, pencils and pencil sharpeners. These are the kind of things that are taken for granted by a great number of (but by no means all) children in wealthy nations but not by many in Eastern Europe, Africa and Asia where they are distributed to those in greatest need. Among those who support the project are those who make soft toys, scour the shops again and again for suitable items, wrap and fill boxes and donate generously. There is another project in my area run by local churches providing a refuge for those living on the streets where they can get a meal, a shower, medical advice, a listening ear and time in a warm, dry place. Many reading these words will know of other similar projects where Tabitha's way of serving is making good things happen.

Of course Tabitha on her own could not meet all the needs of those in her community. However, when faced with the choice between doing something rather than nothing she had a look at her skillset and decided that making clothes for those in need was something she just had to do. But of course she wasn't working on her own. In the course of preparing to visit Timişoara, Romania as part of the charity project referred to in an earlier study I attended a conference in London and met and listened to people involved in many other projects to help a country that had only recently been freed from pretty brutal Communist rule. It helped our team to see that, rather than playing a lone hand, we were a small part of a much bigger effort.

I wonder what happened in Tabitha's life after Peter's visit. She may well have become something of a local celebrity but I'm sure it didn't go to her head; she wasn't that kind of person. Her story challenges us as to whether there is anything more that we could be doing for the needs we see around us. None of us have access to the kind of resources that will transform the entire world but doing nothing is not an option that Jesus leaves open to us. And I get the impression that Tabitha absolutely loved her work which is surely part of the reason why so many people treasured her. Whether we are involved in a shoebox project, helping with a food bank, supporting a local hospice, raising money for charity projects or any one of other myriad ways in which we can work together to make the world more like the Maker intended, we are meant to give and serve joyfully. These tasks are not meant to be onerous (although that does not mean that they aren't hard work!); they are instead deeply fulfilling.

They also have a key role in our discipleship. I'm sure that Tabitha learned a great deal about herself and her walk with God as a result of her project to help clothe the poor of Joppa. Similarly the project in Timișoara was a very steep learning curve for all of us involved. We learned a lot about ourselves, about human nature more generally and, very importantly, about God. It's why being involved in whatever way we can in God's work in the world is such a key part of what it means to be a disciple. It can be tempting to look at the kind of stark inequalities, bitter divisions and antipathy to the Christian faith that increasingly characterise the contemporary world and just throw our arms in the air as if resigned to the fact that nothing we could do will make a blind bit of difference. When we are tempted to feel like that we could do worse than imagine Tabitha in her house spending many hours making a single piece of clothing for one vulnerable widow. For her that one single person really mattered and was worth all the time and effort. It was probably only when she was presented by Peter to the 'believers and widows' (v 41) that she fully understood just how very much her work had been appreciated. But that's not the point; Christian service is not a beauty contest in which we try to impress God or other people, it is quite simply what we do as disciples of Jesus Christ.

Questions: Are we ever tempted to give up in the face of the needs of the world? What more could we be doing?

Prayer: Lord, help us to be active in our discipleship and to be co-workers with you in building your kingdom on earth. Amen.

Ananias: Acts 9:1-19
'Brother Saul' (v 17)

There were two teachers at the school I attended in the sixth form who were known to be atheists. One of them never really mentioned it at all but the other, whose class I was in for French lessons, never missed an opportunity to have a dig at the leader of the school Christian Union! I always felt that the French teacher was the less convincing of the two, as if he needed to keep reinforcing his views by digs at the Christian faith and I wonder if what was going on inside wasn't quite what one saw on the outside.

So as Paul (or 'Saul' as he is known at this point) continues 'breathing out murderous threats against the Lord's disciples' (v 1) I wonder what the real disposition of his heart was? In his own account of his conversion, given when he was on trial in Caesarea, capital of the Roman province of Judaea, he recalls the voice of the risen Jesus questioning his motives for persecuting the church and adding, 'It is hard for you to kick against the goads' (Acts 26:14). The expression describes the way farmers use a stick with a pointed tip to coax a stubborn mule to walk forward. The more the animal kicked against the goad the more likely it was to inflict pain. Paul's activities, undertaken it seems, by one with a picture of Stephen's last moments which he was unable to get out of his head, and which caused such harm to believers were at the same time tearing him apart and just making it hurt more.

Whilst the New Testament tells us a great deal about Paul, both in the book of Acts and through his own writings, Ananias appears only once. He, like Tabitha, is called a disciple but apart from the fact that he lived in Damascus that is pretty much all we know about him. Yet whereas Tabitha was someone who was ministered to by an apostle, Ananias is called to minister to someone who was about to become an apostle. We can identify three key things about Ananias, for convenience they all begin with the same letter.

Firstly there is his *openness to God.* We don't know what form his conversation with God took (v 10–16); it could have been a dream or some kind of vision – we just don't know. Whatever its nature the real point is that Ananias knew what it was that God was asking him to do; he knew whose house he had to go to, he knew who he was going to see and he knew what it was he would be doing. Few of us, I suspect, have very often had that degree of certainty and detail about something God was asking us to do. When facing big decisions, there have been times in my life when even without the level of detail Ananias was furnished with, there has been a certainty that a certain course of action, 'seemed good to the Holy Spirit' (Acts 15:28) and to me. But there have been many other times when I have been less sure and times when I got it badly wrong. I suspect that that uneven track record describes how most of us have fared. Is it merely a question of the nearer we get to God the more often we will know what we should be doing? Well, not necessarily. There were some pretty sharp disagreements in Acts, one of which meant that two key leaders of the early Christian community were unable to continue working together (Acts 15:36-40). One thing we can say, though, is that Ananias seems to have made prayer a priority in his life. Many of us struggle in this area but without it we won't very often be in touch with the inner space which is where we hear the divine voice.

Secondly Ananias *overcame his fear.* Courage is not the absence of fear; it is more about being able to do the right thing in the face of it. None of us, I suspect, have reached the point at which we can fully embrace John's words in his first letter that, 'There is no fear in love. But perfect love drives out fear, because fear has to do with punishment. The one who fears is not made perfect in love' (1 John 4:18). Without doubt it is something to aspire to whilst understanding that we are all works in progress. Ananias questions the will of God here because he is, with much justification, terrified of Saul's reputation. However the point is that he obeys. He may have his heart in his mouth and have trembled at the thought of the encounter that lay ahead but he still turns up at the house of Judas. His actual encounter with Saul reminds me of the famous quote from Mark Twain (which exists in a number of forms), 'I am an old man and have known many troubles, most of them never happened.' We live in an anxious age where it's easy to assume that the worst will happen. No doubt when Ananias actually saw Saul and started speaking to him the relief would have been palpable. It was still very dangerous to be a Christian in Damascus at that time,

Saul or no Saul, and the lesson for Ananias was, as for Peter taking his first steps on the Sea of Galilee, to keep his eyes fixed on Jesus.

Thirdly Ananias was, *otherwise anonymous*, rather like Tabitha. Paul's long and fruitful ministry began literally days after his sight returned and he was baptised (Acts 9:20). The catalyst for this was an almost anonymous disciple who laid his hands on him for his healing and conversion. If we think that there are those in the church (its priests, ministers and pastors) who 'do' ministry as opposed to everybody else who receives it we are off the mark. Sure the church's leaders have had theological and ministerial training but that does not render them either the fount of all wisdom or invulnerable. Although we do it in different ways, everybody in the church gives and receives ministry. Nobody in the church is more or less important than anybody else – every Christian community is a place of universal significance. Every one of us is on a pilgrimage, as was Ananias, and we might sometimes be surprised at what God asks us to do.

I wonder what Ananias thought as word reached him, as it doubtless did, of Paul's exploits as an evangelist or whether he ever got to read any of his letters. I hope he would have been humbled at the small but hugely significant part he played in his story. Through every act of ministry, including every time somebody ministers to someone they would rather have avoided for whatever reason, something happens. What we want to do or feel most comfortable doing isn't necessarily what God is asking us to do (although it might be, of course) which is why we need a perpetual openness to God and to whatever new tasks he calls us to.

Questions: What part has prayer played in the history of our decision making? In what ways does Ananias act as a role model for us?

Prayer: Lord, the desire of our hearts is to do your will. Help us to live prayerfully and to find the inner space to hear your voice calling to us. Amen.

Lydia: Acts 16:11-15; 40
'The Lord opened her heart' (v 14)

I love Charles Dickens's wonderful seasonal novel 'A Christmas Carol' and read it every December in the run up to Christmas. The story of the conversion of Scrooge from mean spirited and hard hearted businessman to generous philanthropist is perhaps the most influential story he ever penned; its publication certainly led to a significant increase in charitable giving. At one point in the story Scrooge is alongside the Ghost of Christmas Present listening to his nephew's wife play a 'simple little air' on the harp and we are told, 'When this strain of music sounded, all the things the Ghost had shown him, came upon his mind; he softened more and more; and thought that if he could have listened to it often, years ago, he might have cultivated the kindnesses of life for his own happiness with his own hands…'. Now we don't need to compare Lydia with Ebenezer Scrooge (apart from the fact that they were both wealthy business owners) but just as the beautiful harp playing opens a door in Scrooge's fictitious heart and leads to profound change so Paul's words, through the grace of God, open Lydia's heart to the good news of Jesus.

Her spiritual journey had been going on for some time. She is described as a 'worshipper of God' (v 14) which means that although she was a Gentile she was sympathetic to the values and beliefs of the Jewish faith without having actually converted to Judaism. The implication of this was that, as far as she was concerned, Paul wasn't starting from scratch. When people become Christians, the interplay between the work of the Holy Spirit and the part played by the new convert is difficult to pin down. Paul makes it clear that Christians shouldn't congratulate themselves for having earned a place among the elect because they made the right response; even the ability to respond to grace is itself a gift of God (Ephesians 2:8). Yet, at the same time, we do need to say 'yes' to God. We don't only do that when we become Christians, of course, as we saw in the previous reflection when considering Ananias – the Christian life involves aligning ourselves with the will of God as a way of life.

What we glean from this riverside encounter is that any response to God's message and his love rests on a work of grace in the human heart. In 'A Christmas Carol' it is the three ghosts who by placing images of the past, present and future before Scrooge work on him bit by bit until he becomes a changed man. In Lydia's case the Holy Spirit, which had already been at work in her heart over a number of years, enables her to see in very sharp focus what had previously been seen from a distance.

It is encouraging to know that when we share our faith with other people it is the Holy Spirit who uses our words, our lifestyle and our prayers to speak to people's hearts. The lifelong process of conversion is a gift of God's grace rather than a purely human endeavour. I think most of us know this but it is worth being reminded from time to time when, for example, we are the only Christian in our workplace, our circle of friends, our class, our WhatsApp or Facebook group or our family, that we are not on our own but that God shares our life journey and, often under the radar, is working gracefully through us by the Spirit.

Of course not everyone will respond positively to the good news. We're told that Lydia, attentively listening, responded to Paul's proclamation of Christ, but we know that there were other women there (v 13) who, it seems, didn't have the same openness. When Paul visited Athens, in spite of him having done his homework and quoting the words of Greek philosophers to back up his message (Acts 17:27-28), the response was not as overwhelming as he might have hoped (although his labours were not entirely fruitless – Acts17:34). Yet such was his faith in the work of the Holy Spirit to change lives that he had to be persuaded to stay with Lydia rather than move on to the next set of encounters that made up the life of an itinerant evangelist. There's nothing at all wrong with inviting people to an event or course at church to unpack the basics of the Christian faith but it's worth remembering that such was Jesus' confidence that God had irreversibly changed the lives of those he healed or set free from evil that, as often as not, he sent them straight home to share with their loved ones what God had done for them!

On that note, it's interesting that without delay (or going on a preparation course) Lydia is baptised along with her household; the Holy Spirit has touched this family which will never be the same again. When Lydia invites Paul and his colleagues to stay with her it is with a certain ambivalence; 'if you consider me to be a believer in the Lord' (v 15). I wonder if this reflects both humility and trepidation as she slightly hesitatingly embraces her new found faith. It's clear that subsequently things moved quickly so that by the end of Paul's rather eventful visit to Philippi, Lydia's house was where a newly formed local Christian community was meeting (v 40). Even as Paul and Silas were being attacked, stripped, beaten and thrown in prison, the Holy Spirit was growing the church.

Of course it isn't just in the area of evangelism that the Holy Spirit is at work in us and through us. As a priest working in a parish context I ministered to people with specific needs on many occasions. This included conducting weddings and funerals and doing lots of listening to people in pain many of whom who did not subsequently become part of a Christian community. Even though many of those people did not join the church I still believe that God was at work in their lives. Just because the person we have been caring for and praying for doesn't start coming along on a Sunday doesn't mean that we have failed God or not demonstrated enough faith. God is at work in all sorts of ways well beyond the church door and I have encountered sincere faith and praying hearts in many who do not attend church on a regular basis. Of course it is very important indeed for Christians to meet for worship as they did at Lydia's house, but we mustn't place limits on how God works and who he is working in and through.

One very good definition of mission states that it is about finding out what God is doing and joining in. The less assumptions we make about how and where the kingdom is being built the more our eyes will be open to the multi-faceted and often surprising work of the Spirit who cannot be made to march to our tune. The church is, of course, an integral part of God's activity in the world yet whenever the hungry are fed, people are released from poverty, conflict ceases, medical advances are made, local communities come together to help those in need and people receive a fair price for what they produce God is just as much at work as he was in the heart of Lydia by the river in Philippi.

Questions: In what way did the Holy Spirit open your heart to the good news of Jesus? What does 'finding out what God is doing and joining in' mean for you?

Prayer: Lord, give us a clearer vision of your Spirit's work in the church and the world and by your grace give us the will to be part of it. Amen.

Bartimaeus: Mark 10:46-52
'Jesus, Son of David,
have mercy on me' (v 47)

I wonder what goes through your mind when you encounter the homeless on the streets of our cities. They are there in increasing numbers and even though for many they are invisible, they are all people with a story to tell. I often wonder when seeing someone sleeping rough what series of events led to the present reality of life on the streets.

It was Bartimaeus' blindness that meant that he was reduced to sitting there day after day by the roadside complete with cloak spread out for the donations he depended on. Unable to support himself and with nobody in the world to look after him, begging was the only option. It meant day after day of humiliation and mockery, of hearing everybody else going about their business and chatting with family and friends while he was locked in a sightless world from which there was no escape. This was all that life was ever going to be – blindness in those days was a one way ticket to isolation. To most people in Jericho on that particular day Bartimaeus might as well have been invisible. Save one.

Jesus was passing through on his way to Jerusalem. He is on the final journey of his earthly life and is about to set off uphill all the way to Jerusalem where he knows that he will suffer and die. He is in a large group of people all on their way to celebrate Passover commemorating the liberation of the people of Israel from slavery in Egypt. Yet in their excitement they walk straight past the man by the roadside enslaved by blindness.

Bartimaeus had got wind of the fact that Jesus was somebody very special, perhaps even that he was able to cure blindness. So when he hears that Jesus is coming past he knows that he has just one shot; it's now or never, slavery or freedom. He screams, 'Jesus, Son of David, have mercy on me' (v 47). He screams and screams and screams even as he is told to shut up and get lost (in all sorts of cruel ways). Jesus stops and in just two words changes the whole of the atmosphere around him. He could have that effect, a bit like when a stone is dropped into a pond and the ripples circle out. In asking those nearby to 'call him' he has communicated to everyone that this beggar is a person and suddenly the abuse he is probably inured to is replaced by encouraging words (v 49b).

Importantly Jesus does not just go ahead and decide what was best for Bartimaeus; he first asks him what he wants him to do for him (v 51). In doing this Jesus treats him with humanity and respect. He wants to see; obvious enough, but when we read the Gospels it is clear that there is more than one way of seeing. There are a number of healings from blindness recorded in the Gospels and these were remembered and thought significant because of the obvious spiritual symbolism embodied in them. This is made most clear in John's Gospel where the healing of a man blind from birth leads to a conversation between Jesus and the Pharisees about spiritual blindness (John 9:35-41). When Jesus heals Bartimaeus, we read that he 'followed Jesus along the road' (v 52). On several occasions in the book of Acts Christianity is described as 'the Way' (Acts 9:2) and the word for 'way' is the same used here for 'road'. We're meant to know that not only was Bartimaeus' physical blindness cured but the eyes of his soul were also opened as he followed Jesus down the road as a new disciple.

If we imagine Jesus coming to us and asking us the same question he asked blind Bartimaeus, how would we answer? What do we want him to do for us? Perhaps we would like to see more clearly the guidance of God, to see and address a habit or attitude that is harming our faith or our relationships with others, to see the truth that is in the Bible in a deeper way or to see more of the love of Jesus. Perhaps there is something else that you would like Jesus to do for you or for someone you love. I can't promise the instant sight giving healing that launched Bartimaeus on his life of discipleship but I do know that your prayer will be heard by one who loves you and respects you very much – our Lord Jesus Christ. We can sometimes feel that, rather like Bartimaeus, we don't matter very much either to God or to other people. It is tempting to think that God has much more important things to worry about than what is on our hearts as we pray. He hasn't. The death of Jesus on the cross holds significance for every single human being who has ever lived or will ever live in the future; and that includes us. We are all loved a very great deal more than we sometimes think.

In considering how desperate Bartimaeus was for Jesus to stop and hear his request I often lament the times when prayer has been put to one side because of something that seemed more urgent or important at the time. That sense that prayer has to be fitted around everything else that makes up day to day life is itself a form of spiritual blindness. I'm aware of how busy people's schedules are and I vividly remember how difficult it was to find quiet moments when there were small children in the house. But if we are to stay close to Jesus we will need to match the urgency that Bartimaeus amply demonstrated in his encounter with him.

Everything in his life changed from that moment. From being totally helpless all kinds of possibilities opened up literally before his eyes. Jesus had recognised his faith and given him the gift of sight in more ways than one. I wish we knew more about what happened in Bartimaeus' journey through life after he followed Jesus down the road. How many others came to believe in Jesus through his testimony? How many people were blessed because they knew him? These are important questions (if unanswerable!) because at the end of the day it wasn't just about him; he didn't receive faith and healing to keep it to himself. Those who follow Jesus on the Way are not members of a private club but a source of blessing for those around them. Those who follow Jesus Christ have something precious to share; the life of God's kingdom. They don't do this by bashing people over the head with a Bible or telling them off when they get it wrong; they do it instead by being the kind of people God wants them to be. I suspect that most Christians have no idea of the way in which they have blessed the lives of those around them or even of those they might have met only briefly. God is at work in all kinds of ways that we don't easily see – another form of blindness! So do be encouraged as you, with Bartimaeus, follow Jesus along the road.

Questions: What is it you would like Jesus to do for you or a loved one today? How can you in the context of your daily life make sure time with God doesn't get squeezed out?

Prayer: Lord Jesus, thank you that everyone matters to you. Help us to live that truth out in our daily lives. Amen.

The Member of the Crowd: Matthew 21:1-11 'Hosanna to the Son of David!' (v 9) (Palm Sunday)

My first visit to Jerusalem in 2013 happened to coincide with Palm Sunday. There was a real hubbub in the Church of the Holy Sepulchre as members of a variety of Christian denominations flourished palm branches to remember Jesus' entry into the city all those years ago. Although it is a day of celebration it is important to bear in mind that the original event, stage managed by Jesus and heavy with symbolism, whilst it was an extraordinary and defining moment, was misunderstood by pretty much everyone present including his disciples.

We're thinking in this reflection about somebody who is unidentified except for the fact that they were present on the first Palm Sunday. In the same way that the unknown soldier represents every soldier who gave their life in World War One, so our unknown and unnamed member of the crowd represents everyone who was there cheering Jesus on his way down the Mount of Olives, across the Kidron Valley and into the city of Jerusalem.

Our anonymous branch waver brought some very particular expectations with her to the event. In her heart was a yearning for freedom from foreign rule stoked by a long-standing hope that a new king, the Messiah, would be the one to bring it about. Her emotions would be running high as it was looking as though Jesus might just be that person. Apart from a short period of freedom following a revolt in the 2nd century BC the people of Israel had been subjected in one way or another for several centuries and at this point in history the province of Judaea was a rather troublesome part of the Roman Empire. Rome had been in charge for quite a while and that wasn't going to change without a major intervention. So, the Messiah's job description involved being the revolutionary leader who would throw out the Romans once and for all. Raising people's expectations is an uncertain business at the best of times bringing with it the risk of a big let-down if, for example, your team loses the cup final or the much-anticipated movie isn't all it's cracked up to be. But what if, as was the case here, what Jesus had to come to do was nothing like what the crowd had in mind?

Matthew quotes Old Testament prophecy (Zechariah 9:9) to make the point that, although Jesus did self-consciously ride into Jerusalem as a king, it was with humility and gentleness rather than as a conquering hero. If we read the following verse in Zechariah, it's clear that Matthew wants his readers to understand that Jesus has no intention whatsoever of triggering a conflict but has come to bring peace. As the crowds cry 'Hosanna' (meaning 'save us') to the Son of David' they are addressing one who has indeed come to save, just not in the sense that they were hoping and expecting. It was only a few days later that another very angry crowd was crying out 'Crucify him' and being nailed to a Roman cross was most certainly not part of the Messiah's job description.

Jesus was a severe disappointment to many of the people of Jerusalem; a failure rather than a prophet, king and Messiah, the call to crucify reflecting the kind of dashed hopes which very often boil over in anger and frustration. Yet those hopes had to be disappointed if the real work that Jesus had come to do was to be accomplished. Military victory, with its attendant suffering, bloodshed and death would only, as it always has done, have led to further suffering in the future with one conflict leading inevitably to another (that was certainly the way of things in the Roman Empire). When Jesus died on the cross, he gave his life non-violently for the sins of the world whilst praying for the forgiveness of those who had put him there. This was completely inexplicable to everyone else in Jerusalem that week, including those who knew him and loved him well. As far as his followers were concerned, despite having been warned by Jesus several times about this turn of events, they are left completely shattered.

How have you managed your expectations of the Christian life? I wonder if there have been any occasions when you have been disappointed (or even shattered) by Jesus not doing what you so wanted or expected him to do? Has a prayer for healing, whether for yourself or another person, seemingly remained unanswered? Have you had a painful experience that your faith cannot seem to compute? Has that initial enthusiasm you had for a newfound Christian faith cooled somewhat over the years until, if you're honest, following Jesus has become a bit of a struggle?

I don't have the answer to these questions and certainly don't have full explanations as to why some prayers seem to go unanswered or some of our hopes are dashed. But it certainly isn't because our faith isn't good enough, we've done something wrong, or God has given up on us. When we follow Jesus to the cross, we see a depth of love for all of humanity that may not answer all our questions yet is still compelling. And, of course, if the story had ended on Good Friday, then, as Paul puts it, 'our preaching is useless, and so is your faith' (1 Corinthians 15:14). It is the resurrection that demonstrates that everything Jesus said about himself is true and that it was the real Messiah who entered Jerusalem on a donkey on Palm Sunday. Although not a single person was able to see it at the time, Jesus was doing exactly what he came to do with the kind of salvation he offered being firmly grounded in the sacrifice he made with such love and patient suffering.

In many churches palm crosses are distributed on Palm Sunday as a reminder of the reason Jesus entered the city. Jesus was utterly good, holy, loving, and generous in a way that those who would cause him such suffering found threatening. Speaking truth to power is always a risky business. One is tempted to say that there was an inevitability about where the story was heading. But although people jeered rather than cheered as Jesus went to the cross it was, in complete contrast to what it seemed to be, a moment of victory and vindication. In his death and resurrection, he dealt with the potency of sin and reconciled humanity to God. It was the victory of life and the defeat of death.

And it is the scope of that love that is breath-taking; Jesus didn't give his life as part of a national struggle, he gave his life for all, announcing that every human being is now invited to the party in the kingdom of God – no wonder it's good news! This means that we can fully share in the excitement of the many pilgrims in the Church of the Holy Sepulchre. We can find joy in the knowledge that, because of the one who rode humbly and gently on a donkey, there will be a new heaven and a new earth in which our hopes will be fulfilled, and our joy will be endless. Hosanna! Hosanna!

Questions: Have you had any disappointments in your Christian journey (such as prayers seemingly not answered)? How have you responded and what impact have they had on your faith?

Prayer: Lord Jesus, as we see you riding into the city help us to remember with thankfulness, amidst the excitement of Palm Sunday, that you gave your life for us all. Amen.

The Widow at the Temple:
Mark 12:41-44 'She, out of her poverty, put in everything' (v 44)

Jesus is in the last week of his earthly life, and we are faced with a profoundly uncomfortable reading. A former colleague of mine suggested that whereas the Communion service in the Book of Common Prayer has some 'comfortable words' of Jesus after the confession and absolution, it might be better if there were some uncomfortable words! Plenty of what Jesus had to say presents some pretty tough challenges to all of us.

Many of us, me included, give knowing that we have enough to fall back on to keep a roof over our heads and provide us with enough food to eat. We give to our local church, to organisations such as Christian Aid who work with the poorest and most vulnerable communities across the globe and volunteer our help when there is an initiative to help the needy. Yet we are not paying the catastrophic price that the widow does as she drops the only two coins she has into the Temple treasury. What is she going to eat for the rest of the day? Where is she going to find any money for her future needs? In the absence of social security and with no breadwinner to rely on she has just dropped today's food and drink into the box. There is nothing left.

There is just one occasion when Jesus challenges somebody to give everything they possess away. The rich young man who approaches Jesus with a question about how to inherit eternal life is told that to follow him he must give everything to the poor (Mark 10:17-22). The one time somebody leaves Jesus with his head down is because of love of money. Of course, it's clear that Jesus didn't demand that of everybody. Peter had a house in Capernaum which Jesus seems to have used as a base for his Galilean ministry and, before churches started to be built for worship, Christian communities met in people's homes, both very good examples of a generous and welcoming use of property.

Here Jesus is addressing us and all who follow him directly about how much we give and whether there is any cost to us in that giving. That is a challenge that you and I need to hear and respond to. But there is something else going on here. The issue of caring for widows was important in the life of the early church, something we touched on in an earlier reflection. Paul gave some quite detailed instructions about this matter singling out those widows in particular need of special assistance (1 Timothy 5:3-5) whilst acknowledging that there were some who were fine because they had family support and others who were just out for pleasure. The widow whose plight Jesus is drawing to the attention of his disciples to is, it appears, entirely on her own and completely destitute.

The question that springs readily to mind is why she is feeling any obligation to give when she should be receiving assistance from the very organisation receiving her last two coins? One reason is the eternal truism that the less people have the more generous they are. This is partly because those who are in need themselves tend to have more empathy for others in similar circumstances than those who have never wanted for anything. The widow is giving because, being in need herself, she has a keen awareness of the needs of others and wants to contribute. Those who have only known luxury have never had to worry about any of their needs being met and in fact might be inclined to regard luxuries beyond the reach of most people as needs in the context of their lifestyle. It's very easy to get wants and needs mixed up! This, it must be said, doesn't mean that wealthy people are not capable of generosity; the Bill and Melinda Gates Foundation does amazing work among the poorest communities on the planet with some of the vast sums of money made by the co-founder of Microsoft. It's just that this kind of philanthropy, whilst impressive, will never make those who sponsor it anything other than extremely wealthy.

I wonder also whether, back at the Temple, the ostentatious giving that rich people were indulging in was creating pressure in the widow's mind to follow suit. I suspect once they had put their bags of money into the treasury, they didn't give it another thought and felt satisfied that they had fulfilled their obligations. But what about a widow with only a couple of coins? How is she to respond to this heap of money being given? Imagine it's Sunday morning in church and the collection plate is coming round (a practice thankfully being abolished in many churches). On one row there are several well-heeled people all with wallets stuffed with twenty-pound notes. They each open their wallets and place a couple of them in the plate. At the end of the row is someone hard up who, getting more and more uncomfortable as the plate comes down the row, feels obliged to place all she has with her, the cost of her bus fare home, in the plate. It's a caricature, of course, and doesn't do the original justice but the criticism that Amos makes of those who 'brag about your freewill offerings' (Amos 4:5) has some relevance here.

So, the widow stands for us not only as a challenge to give generously but to ensure that the church is a place committed to making poverty history. Wouldn't it have been great if the Temple, as part of its ministry, had done more to look after people like this widow, rather in the way that Pope Francis has made hot showers and free underwear available at the Vatican for the use of homeless people, rather than asking them to give their last penny?

Giving is sometimes thought of as an onerous duty and nobody looks forward to the annual Sunday sermon when the vicar or the treasurer gets up to encourage those who can to give more. Yet the New Testament presents giving as one of the great joys of the Christian life. Paul writes, 'Each of you should give what you have decided in your heart to give, not reluctantly or under compulsion, for God loves a cheerful giver' (2 Corinthians 9:7). This means that giving is, according to their ability to do so, something that Christians should love doing. But Paul very importantly says that it isn't something that should be done under compulsion. Nobody should feel that they must render themselves destitute and part of the joy of giving is that it helps lift people out of poverty providing them and their families with hope and a future. There are so many opportunities to give these days; you can even twin your loo by funding the building of a toilet and access to clean water in a community in Africa or Asia (www.toilettwinning.org). Organisations such as Christian Aid, The Leprosy Mission, The Children's Society, The Trussell Trust and heaps of others working locally (not forgetting that there is much need on our doorstep), nationally and globally are doing great work and inviting us to join in.

I'm sure many reading these words give generously and support much wonderful work. But it's good from time to time to do an audit and see what more we might do to add to our own joy as givers and the subsequent joy of those who receive as a result. As the gap between rich and poor widens exponentially Christians should be active among those who are working to close the gap. That yawning gulf existed two thousand years ago in Jerusalem when it was challenged by Jesus watching a widow give all she had in the world after all the affluent donors went home to their lives of plenty feeling they had done their bit.

It is a task that will never be finished so one that presents a perpetual challenge but which, if we could but see it, offers great gladness.

Questions: Have you thought of giving as a joy or a bit of a chore? Why is it important that Christians who have the resources should be generous?

Prayer: Lord Jesus, you gave everything you had for us, help us to be generous as we respond to your love and the needs of so many in our community, nation, and world. Amen.

The Spies: Luke 20:20-26
'They were unable to trap him' (v 26)

We're all familiar with the way that politicians sometimes give evasive answers to direct questions; it's one of the things that breeds cynicism about them. The problem with the question that Jesus is faced with in our passage is that it is not a genuine one. We might wonder if it was thought up by a committee set up to come up with a question that would be impossible for Jesus to answer without getting into hot water one way or another. What gives this extra bite is that the intention is not just to undermine him or to make him look foolish. The chief priests want to kill him and are looking for evidence that they can use to have him convicted. It is Jesus' life that is at stake here.

The inquisitors begin by buttering him up before setting the trap (v 21), something he would have seen through so easily it was hardly worth the bother. Payment of tax to Caesar was a political hot potato, not just because the Jewish people hated handing money over to their Roman overlords but also because the coins used for this purpose bore the image of Caesar, which was in itself considered idolatrous, but was compounded by the fact that the wording asserted the divinity of Roman emperors. Although this will slowly change following her death, if you look at a British pound coin, you will see the late Queen's head with 'ELIZABETH II D G REG F D' around the outside. This stands for 'Elizabeth II Dei Gratia Regina Fidei Defensor' or in English, 'Elizabeth the second, by the grace of God, Queen, Defender of the Faith (the faith being that of the Church of England of which she was the Supreme Governor). The writing around the outside of the tribute coin that Jews in Jesus' time were obliged to use to pay the tax to Caesar described him as 'the son of the divine Augustus'. To the Jewish people who believed in one God this was complete anathema.

And here's the trap. On the one hand if Jesus tells them that they should pay the tax he'll be accused of disloyalty not just to the nation but ultimately to God.

On the other hand, if he tells them to withhold the tax he can then be arrested, taken to the Roman governor, and accused of being a revolutionary. Got him!

Except they haven't. He asks them to produce one of the coins in question which, rather embarrassingly, exposes the fact that they themselves are using them. The intentionally enigmatic answer to the question as to whether people should pay taxes to Caesar is that you should give to Caesar what is rightfully his whilst also giving God what is due to him. The trap has been sprung and some more head scratching is going to be needed if they are to get Jesus to incriminate himself.

It goes without saying that, as the Son of God himself, Jesus would have known that the claim of the Caesars to divinity was empty and blasphemous because there is only one God whose authority he embodies. Indeed, at the end of Matthew's Gospel the risen Jesus says to his disciples, 'All authority in heaven and on earth has been given to me' (Matthew 28:18). Whilst he wasn't going to be drawn into the duplicitous strategies that this question formed just one element of (Luke 20:19), it should have been clear to anyone listening that Jesus is saying that it is to God rather than Caesar that loyalty is owed – just not in so many words.

That means that it isn't a competition with governments and God battling it out for our loyalty. Paul helps us out here when he says, 'Let everyone be subject to the governing authorities, for there is no authority except that which God has established. The authorities that exist have been established by God' (Romans 13:1). This means that states and governments only have a derivative authority meaning that political leaders are servants rather than masters. The idea of 'public service', which is not talked about much these days, expresses a profound truth about those in authority. Whether they know it or understand it or not, those who govern us are God's servants.

So, what about the totalitarian dictatorships, the cruel regimes and the corrupt leaders that, if anything, seem to be on the rise in the early twenty first century? What about those governments that deny people justice and imprison, torture and kill their critics? When Paul argues that if we rebel against authority we are rebelling against God (Romans 13:2) does that mean we have to accept all the injustice and cruelty without so much as a whimper?

It most certainly doesn't; because when those in authority go beyond their God given brief to govern wisely and for the public good, loyalty to God must come first. When the apostles are arrested by the Jewish authorities for preaching the good news of Jesus and are told in no uncertain terms to stop doing it, they reply simply and honestly, 'We must obey God rather than human beings' (Acts 5:29). Christians living under regimes that persecute and prosecute them for their faith have a higher loyalty, which often comes at a heavy cost for them and their loved ones. On a wider canvas those of all faiths and none who speak out against corrupt and autocratic governance often do so at great personal risk. The passage quoted above from Acts is about doing the right thing even if that involves the risky business of challenging those wielding power in a way that exceeds their God given authority (Romans 13:3-4).

Loyalty to God also means that it is right and proper to protest about issues of justice and peace. It's entirely right and proper, for example, to put pressure on governments over the issue of climate change. One responsibility that God gives to all those in authority in every nation is to look after the planet and if they are not doing their job somebody has to let them know! We might have different views about the way that 'Extinction Rebellion' protestors have blocked roads and otherwise inconvenienced people as part of their protest, but we would agree, I think, that there is an urgency about this matter that requires people in government (and everybody else, of course) to get the message.

On the other hand, the coronavirus lockdown restrictions that we became very familiar with were, although frustrating and often distressing, very much for the common good and it was right that we observed them. To protect the population and keep them safe is very clearly a God given responsibility that falls to those in authority. This means that in failing to social distance or wear masks people were resisting an authority that ultimately derives from God's compassionate love for humanity. That's why it is important that we pay our taxes (and personally I would like to pay more) so that, as a society, we can better care for the sick, vulnerable, and needy and those who look after them so selflessly.

Balancing our loyalty to God with our obligations as citizens is not an exact science. Christians don't always (or often!) agree with one another about such things as the size of the state and the limits of its responsibilities. What I think Jesus is saying, even enigmatically, in his answer to the spies is that our ultimate loyalty must be to God and that it is our identity as his people rather than any national identity that ultimately defines who we are.

Questions: What do you think it means to 'render unto the authorities what belongs to the authorities and to God what belongs to God' in today's world? Are there any potential conflicts for you between these two obligations?

Prayer: Lord, we pray for those who govern us, that they may do so wisely and for the common good especially when difficult decisions need to be made. Amen.

The Woman with the Alabaster Jar: Matthew 26:6-13
'You will not always have me' (v 11)

Today's reading describes a moment of beauty sandwiched between ugliness. The passage is preceded by developments in the plot to kill Jesus and followed by Judas going to the chief priests and being offered his thirty pieces of silver. It is getting very dark, but we have in the story of the woman with the alabaster jar a moment of light which, whilst it foreshadows Jesus' death (v 12), radiates love and devotion in an intensely moving way. In the parallel account in John's Gospel the woman is identified as Mary, the sister of Martha and Lazarus, who we last saw sitting at the feet of Jesus while her sister got hot and bothered. However, as she is not named in Matthew's account we'll leave her identity, as he does, to one side.

We don't know whether the act of pouring perfume on Jesus' head was something she had long planned or whether it was an impulse, done on the spur of the moment for someone who had clearly changed her life so very much. As he faces intense suffering Jesus accepts the gift and the love that it represents even in the face of criticism from the disciples. But here's the rub; the perfume was expensive and could indeed have been sold to help the poor. In ordinary circumstances we would admit that the disciples had a point and would certainly applaud somebody who sold an expensive possession and gave the proceeds to charity.

These are not ordinary times, though, and as the perfume drips down his body Jesus seems both to accept the death that is only a few days away and to sense that the meaning of this act reaches beyond the moment to be part of the proclamation of the good news about him (v 12–13). Jesus was the Son of God, but he was also a human being and facing the horror of what lay ahead was far from easy, as we know from his agonised pleading in the Garden of Gethsemane later in the same chapter (Matthew 26:38-44). The body that was now being anointed would, a couple of days hence, be flogged and hung on a cross. Jesus would find himself surrounded by his enemies, pierced by nails and a sword, and hung up to die. I wonder whether, as he suffered on the cross, he recalled the perfume and the devotion it represented and it helped him.

In this context we begin to understand Jesus' difficult saying in answer to the criticism of the disciples that, 'The poor you will always have with you, but you will not always have me' (v 11). Jesus doesn't say this in a sort of world weary and cynical way; after all he had spent his whole ministry caring for, healing, and giving hope to the poor, destitute and excluded. Nobody cared more for the poor than Jesus. Yet for Jesus the time to say goodbye was near. He would not be physically with them for much longer. By Friday he would be in a tomb. On Sunday he would rise from death, and someone called Mary would try to cling to him in the garden only to be told that he must return to his Father and she must let go (John 20:17). Jesus accepts this oil as a token of love, in a way, as a farewell gift knowing that the work of caring for the poor will be a central feature of the future ministry of his Spirit inspired people as they build the kingdom on earth to make it look more like heaven. Here a moment is seized that doesn't set any kind of precedent but has a particular and potent meaning in the shadow of the cross.

And it is a moment of costly devotion. The perfume was indeed expensive and even though it wasn't sold and used to help the poor it still represented a significant personal sacrifice. It helps us to reflect on the cost of our devotion to Jesus. He had earlier told his disciples that 'those who do not carry their cross and follow me cannot be my disciples' (Luke 14:27). Ouch! I don't think Jesus is saying that the intense pain he experienced when he carried the cross should be normative for Christians all the time; after all, when he said it, he hadn't experienced that pain himself. Jesus says later in the same passage that the cost of discipleship involves 'giving up everything' (Luke 14:33). We need to sift his meaning carefully, bearing in mind that he had earlier gone as far as speaking hyperbolically of hating family members and even our own lives if we are to be his disciples (Luke 14:26). It's an example of a figure of speech to make the point – of course we are to love our families (and ourselves; often the difficult bit) but we will be able to do that much more genuinely if our commitment to Jesus is absolute. If our faith in Jesus is to be at the heart of our thinking, speaking, and doing it will mean quite a lot of costly giving up, which is what taking up the cross means here. So, as we grow in faith, we increasingly take leave of a life built around our own desires and ambitions and embrace the profoundly transformative process of prayerfully finding God's will for our lives. As our worlds cease to revolve around ourselves and we respond to the call to reflect the love of our creator in our thoughts, words and deeds we will discover what it means to be an authentic human being. This is a particularly difficult thing to do in a consumer society where we're constantly being told that we should buy products 'because we're worth it' (or words to that effect).

The woman with the alabaster jar is so significant because she loved Jesus enough to be prepared to give him a gift at great expense. She gave something up for him. She reminds us that faith is not meant to be an optional extra, a sort of palliative medicine to make the hurly burly of life a bit more bearable. It is a commitment that, as has been said many times, is free yet costs everything. But what we then receive is life in all its fullness. Our sacred vocation as human beings is to live in the loving embrace of our creator, share our faith, serve our fellow human beings and care for creation and when we do these things we become more and more, little by little, the people we were always meant to be.

The starting point is responding to the astonishing sacrificial love that Jesus displays in giving his life for us. The final verse of Isaac Watts' wonderful hymn 'When I survey the wondrous cross' could have been written by the woman with alabaster jar and challenges us to respond with costly devotion to the one who gave us all he had.

> Were the whole realm of nature mine,
> That were an offering far too small;
> Love so amazing, so divine,
> Demands my soul, my life, my all.

Questions: if you had been in the room when the perfume was poured on Jesus' head what would you have thought? What do Jesus' words about taking up the cross mean to you?

Prayer: Forbid it, Lord, that I should boast, save in your death for me. All the vain things that charm me most, I sacrifice them to your blood. Amen.

The Disciple Whom Jesus Loved: John 13:1-30 'Lord, who is it?' (v 25) (Maundy Thursday)

All of us have special people in our lives; our closest family and friends, those with whom we have a very special bond. It shouldn't therefore be a surprise that 'the disciple whom Jesus loved' had a particularly close and warm relationship with him. This disciple isn't mentioned very often and all his appearances, of which this is the first, are towards the end of John's Gospel. His identification with the writer of John (or at least the written testimony on which the book is based) has led many to conclude that he is John himself but there can be no certainty about this.

The occasion for today's reading is the Last Supper. John does not actually describe the meal as such, but it is without doubt the same occasion. By washing the disciples' feet – something they were extremely uncomfortable with – Jesus illustrated the nature of his own servant ministry as well as providing them with an example to follow in their own future Christian service.

Then comes the bombshell; there is a betrayer in the house. The shock is palpable. They obviously want to know who it is and Peter, rather than making an approach himself, has a word with the beloved disciple about asking Jesus to identify the traitor, which he duly does. I think we must imagine a febrile atmosphere with all sorts of loud conversations going on with people talking across one another left, right and centre. Peter may well have asked the beloved disciple to find out who it was simply because he was the one sitting next to Jesus meaning that all he had to do was lean back and quietly whisper the question. During the hubbub Judas is identified by Jesus and leaves before the disciples have had a chance to understand what is going on.

I wonder also whether Peter asks the beloved disciple because, given his bond of friendship with Jesus, he considered him above suspicion. Of course, it wasn't only Judas that was to betray Jesus that night; Peter was also about to have the most traumatic moral failure of his life thus far as Jesus is arrested and he finds himself, racked with fear for his own life, unable to admit to any association with him. This was a traumatic night for everybody; even Jesus himself recoils in terror from what he is being asked to do in his dark night of the soul in the Garden of Gethsemane.

On a night when Jesus pleaded, Judas was on the make and Peter lost his bottle it seems that everything that the disciples thought they knew was being turned upside down. It was one thing to follow Jesus around Galilee watching him teach and heal but the trauma of his arrest put into question everything they had lived for over the past three years or so. They might well have been asking themselves whether they were all mistaken about Jesus and, just as urgently if not more so, whether it was going to cost them their lives.

There are moments in our lives when we question everything we thought we knew. An event that we didn't see coming; a medical diagnosis, a bereavement, the breakdown of a relationship, the loss of a job or even (or especially) a pandemic can make us ask questions that we didn't know needed answering and cause us mental, emotional, and spiritual distress. If we are Christians, it can lead us to seriously question our faith. How could God have allowed this to happen? Where was he when I needed him? Why doesn't he answer my prayers? What hope is there for the future?

It's important to remember that these were the sort of questions the disciples, including the beloved disciple, were asking that dark night. For him Jesus was a greatly loved friend, mentor, guide, and teacher. To find that Judas was not who he appeared to be was difficult to deal with in itself but the heartbreak of seeing Jesus being crucified must have felt like having his own hands and feet pierced. Yet he was there when Jesus died, the beloved friend and follower to whom Jesus entrusts his mother (John 19:26-27). Whilst fully sharing the fear and confusion of his fellow disciples he had nevertheless sought out Jesus' mother and accompanied her to the cross despite the cost to him of doing so.

The beloved disciple provides an example of faith, love and loyalty that is so deeply rooted that even when life threw at him the worst that could possibly happen, he wasn't so overwhelmed that he ran for his life without so much as a glance over his shoulder. The cost of seeing the back that he had leaned against a couple of days before raw from flogging against the rough wood of the cross was enormous, yet his integrity remained intact, something recognised by Jesus in his request. He was still the reliable and loving friend even though he too must have thought that his own life was falling apart. It's no coincidence that when he and Peter ran to Jesus' tomb on the Sunday morning that the instant he caught sight of the strips of linen and burial cloth folded up 'he saw and believed' (John 20:8). It suggests to me that he had never quite given up, that there was a place in the depths of his heart that was waiting for something like this; a sign of hope that it had not just all ended in failure. He so wanted there to be more to the future than trying to pick up the pieces and carry on with a life that had lost all meaning.

I've talked with many people over the years who have come to a point in their lives when they have seriously questioned or even abandoned their faith. I wonder if the beloved disciple offers us a way of continuing to embrace our faith even though we may feel there isn't much evidence that God is around or interested in us. We may sometimes feel that God is conspicuously silent, yet we can find reassurance in the story of this loving follower who had a faith that survived somewhere in the deep places of his heart which is where God's often wordless presence is to be found.

It took a lot to keep even a sliver a faith alive when Jesus was arrested and crucified and Judas was certainly one who couldn't compute what was happening. There are those who believe that he had links with zealots who believed that armed insurgence was the only way forward and that when Jesus talked about suffering and dying something within him snapped and his faith that Jesus was leading him down the right path evaporated. Yet suffering and dying are integral parts of our faith. Being a Christian doesn't mean that only good things will happen to us or that there will never be moments of doubt, confusion, pain, and loss. What we do know is that they never speak the final word. That final word, as the beloved disciple well knew, is love; and because Christ rose from death and he found himself able to see and believe, so we can look forward to a time when, in the words of St Augustine:

'All shall be Amen and Alleluia.
We shall rest and we shall see.
We shall see and we shall know.
We shall know and we shall love.
We shall love and we shall praise.
Behold our end which is no end.'

Questions: Have there been times in your own life when events have made you question your faith? How can we keep the faith at such times?

Prayer: Lord Jesus, as we reflect on the terrible events that led to your death help us to see the thread of love that runs through them as you walk the way of the cross for us. Amen.

The Repentant Criminal: Luke 23:32; 39-43 'Today you will be with me in paradise' (v 43) (Good Friday)

Crucifixion was a brutal, humiliating and very common method of execution in the Roman Empire. It served as a method of concentrating the minds of those who might be tempted to indulge in anything from common criminality to challenging the might of the Roman Empire. Crucifixions were carried out very deliberately on main roads into towns and occupied crosses were therefore very visible to all those entering and leaving.

In our reading there are three men each on a cross fighting for breath. They all know that they are soon to die. One of them has a mocking sign above his head saying, 'this is the king of the Jews'. The other two are criminals. One of them adds his own insults; default behaviour for those being crucified. The other one looks across and, right at its end, makes the most important discovery of his life. One of the very significant things that Luke wants us to know through his telling of the story is that Jesus, even as he dies the death of a criminal, is completely innocent. So it is that he includes the testimony of the centurion standing by Jesus' cross who says of him, 'Surely this was a righteous man' (Luke 23:47) as well as words of Jesus himself who prays from the cross for those who have been complicit in his death (Luke 23:34). This is a good man who is being executed and the repentant criminal can see it.

The criminal sees his own guilt against the innocence of the man hanging next to him. In recording his words Luke intends him to speak for the rest of us as Jesus, the completely innocent one, dies on the cross for the sins of humanity. In a real sense we share the guilt of the criminal and so it is also to us that Jesus offers forgiveness and a place with him in paradise (v 43). Here the story of Jesus coming into the world to reconcile humanity to God reaches its defining moment.

We have seen throughout these meanderings along the Bible's back roads that human beings are capable of great things. As we have passed by, we have noted Jonathan's selfless loyalty to his friend David, Esther's bravery and resourcefulness in a very scary situation and Joseph's thoughtful and sensitive regard for Mary's welfare even when it looked like she had betrayed him. But we have also seen Cain's murderous intent, David's calculating methods of getting what he wanted and the spies' barbed questions to try and trap Jesus. We are such a mixed bag! In addition, many of the people we have considered, such as the paralysed man, the woman at the well, the widow of Nain and Bartimaeus have undergone significant transformation in one way or another.

Whilst we are capable of so much good, which does need to be celebrated, we have also failed to fulfil our vocation as those made in God's image to honour him and respond to his love because too often we don't live our lives in the way that we are meant to. Human beings tend to put themselves first far too often and sometimes don't do a very good job of caring for one another; especially the lonely, the vulnerable and those in pain. In our generation, too much greed and selfishness mean that the beautiful planet we have been asked to care for is hurting. Too often we go into 'us and them' mode, failing to even begin to understand what it is like being the other person. Yet none of us would want to live in a world in which behaving selfishly, cruelly, and thoughtlessly do not matter; a world without morality is unthinkable.

God does not and cannot stop loving this world and everybody in it which is why there was an innocent man hanging alongside a guilty one offering him a place in paradise. Our representative on the cross clearly has some kind of moral compass, which is why he recognises the innocence of Jesus. Yet things have also gone wrong in his life, and he has got himself into trouble. He understands his need for redemption.

As Jesus dies he washes away the sins of humanity in a tidal wave of divine love which restores us, reconciles us to God and leads to the creation of a new heaven and earth where suffering and death will be no more. It isn't that God's anger had to be taken out on somebody, so he sent Jesus to take the rap or that what Jesus did made God suddenly change his mind about us. The Christian faith is about God loving us so much that he sent his only and beloved Son to die for our sins on the cross and to rise from death to assure us that there is nothing that can separate us from the reality of that love now or in eternity.

This means that the sins of those who put Jesus on his cross; those who plotted his death, those who told lies about him, those who sentenced him to death, those who flogged and beat him, those who mocked him and those who nailed him to the cross are made as nothing such is the depth and power of his love. That is precisely why Jesus prays for their forgiveness. By being hated and offering only love in return Jesus declares that love is infinitely more powerful than hate, light will inevitably overcome all darkness and life will triumph over death. This is why Christianity is such good news.

And it is still good news! Jesus died on the cross to wash away the sins of the repentant criminal and the rest of humanity who stand in solidarity with him in his need for forgiveness. He came to show us that God loves every one of us as we are and longs for us to be healed and whole. He came to bring into this world the kingdom of God in which there is justice, peace, and goodness. He came to share an amazing hope that death is not the final act of the human story but is, in a wonderful way, only the beginning.

These are powerful truths that we are called to embrace and live out. It may be that Christianity is being pushed to the margins in many societies and that secular assumptions increasingly form the thinking of many. But God, in Jesus Christ, still ceaselessly addresses the world with the words 'I love you' as he always will. God has not given up on the world and he calls us, as those who believe in the forgiveness of sins and eternal life, to be witnesses to the sacred truths we share.

The repentant criminal had probably only met Jesus as they were being nailed to their respective crosses. So, this was the first time they had spoken to each other. It is because there isn't much time left (Jesus dies much earlier than the soldiers were expecting) that his offer of 'paradise' is gasped out so quickly. Paradise is a word that derives from Persian and refers to a garden, enclosure, or park. It is a place where there is no suffering, where there is complete peace and tranquillity and, we would add, based on Jesus' offer, where his presence is known for ever.

In terms of our own relationship with Jesus, perhaps we speak with him every day in our prayers, perhaps we mean to or don't quite manage to do it or perhaps we haven't, if we're being honest, spoken with him in a while. Let his words of assurance to the repentant criminal personally address you now and maybe lead to a conversation with him. Luke means all of us to hear them and know that they are as true for us as for the man who died with Jesus that day.

Wherever we are in life now and whatever the state of our faith Jesus never stops calling to us. He doesn't just see us as we are with all our faults and imperfections, he sees what we might be, indeed what we will be in his glory. We are graciously invited to kneel at the cross and accept the unconditional forgiveness Jesus offers all of us for the times we get it wrong. He doesn't want us to grovel in the dirt before him, he wants us to look up into his eyes and know ourselves to be set free from all that pulls us down or lies to us that we are worth nothing. The stories of the people who have appeared on the back roads of the Bible converge with our stories at the cross of Christ. Here it is that God's love for the world and for everyone who has walked its roads is made fully visible.

Questions: What does the death of Jesus mean to you? What do you want to say to him today?

Prayer: Lord Jesus, thank you that you gave your life for us all. As we ask for forgiveness fill us with new life and purpose. Amen.

Joseph of Arimathea: Luke 23:50-56
'He asked for Jesus' body' (v 52)

When I was training for ordained ministry, I was involved in a series of three assemblies at a local school. We decided to imagine that there had been television news broadcasts in Palestine at the time of Jesus (about 1900 years before the first actual broadcast was made!) complete with a newsreader and a reporter who interviewed further members of our team dressed as characters in the story. The first assembly focused on the Friday of Jesus' crucifixion, the second on the Saturday after the crucifixion and the third on the Sunday Jesus rose from the dead. For the Saturday report one of the team came on stage completely covered in blankets. He was acting the part of one of Jesus' disciples who had gone into hiding and he told the reporter how all his hopes and dreams had been shattered and he was now frightened for his life. For the third assembly the same team member, minus the blankets and in ordinary clothes, testified to the complete transformation that had taken place because Jesus was alive again. The point of the assemblies was to get across the profound change in mood which took place between the Friday and Sunday of Holy Week making sure not to leave the Saturday out. We enjoyed doing the assemblies and I hope the school students liked them too!

We sometimes don't give much thought to the Saturday between Good Friday and Easter Sunday, but today's reading reminds us just how traumatic the Sabbath between Jesus' crucifixion and resurrection was. There were no more hopes and dreams for his friends and followers; just the despair of seeing, as they thought, everything they had built those hopes and dreams on crumble before their eyes. It must have been an unbearable day.

Joseph of Arimathea shared the grief of Jesus' followers. He was a member of the Jewish Council who was 'waiting for the kingdom of God' (v 51). Right at the beginning of his life, the infant Jesus met Simeon, someone else who was waiting (Luke 2:25), meaning that Jesus' life was bookended by encounters with people living expectantly. Joseph was a member of the establishment to his fingertips and yet had publicly disagreed with the actions of his colleagues in condemning Jesus at his trial. He would certainly have raised the suspicions of his colleagues that he was a fifth columnist.

So, to go to Pilate and ask for Jesus' body, once again publicly identifying himself with him was very risky indeed. In Mark's account of his request, he adds that he went boldly (literally 'taking courage' – Mark 15:43). It's as if he thought through the possible consequences, took a deep breath, and asked to see Pilate. The bravery and devotion of this man with a lot to lose is an inspiration. Just as rough and unfeeling hands nailed Jesus to his cross, so loving hands take him down, wrap his body and place him in his tomb. Because of the rocky terrain it was not possible to bury bodies under the ground. Instead, bodies were placed in caves or, as in the case of Jesus, a specially constructed tomb that had been cut out of the rock. These were often large enough to accommodate several bodies hence Luke's note that Jesus' was the first body to be buried there (v 53). Having placed him in his tomb Joseph then rolls the stone across its door (Mark 15:46). It was an extremely big stone and even though we know from John's account that Nicodemus was there to help (John 19:39), extra hands would certainly have been needed.

Joseph, whether he is aware of it or not, is being followed. The Galilean women who are keeping tabs on him had been with Jesus from the beginning. They too are brave and devoted and having noted which tomb Joseph had placed Jesus in, they go to prepare spices to anoint his body. It's important to keep in mind that Joseph and the women were preparing his body for burial rather than resurrection (v 55–56). There would have been many tears as they watched Joseph perform his melancholy duty. Whereas they once had a teacher who was more alive than anyone else they had ever met, all they had now was a body. Even though we know how the story ends (or in reality has no ending) we share the profound sadness. And the Sabbath was about to begin.

I was once present at the Western Wall in Jerusalem for the eve of Sabbath celebrations. The enormous crowds and scenes of celebration were quite extraordinary. There was singing, cheering, and dancing and the exhilarating party atmosphere was like nothing I'd ever experienced before. The fact that the best day of the week, the day when there was no work giving everyone a chance to rest and celebrate, was about to begin throws the despair of Joseph, the women from Galilee and the disciples (wherever they were) into stark relief. They were not even able to busy themselves to take their minds off the numbing sense of grief; all they could do, pretty much literally, was to sit there.

There are times in all our lives when we grieve the loss of a loved one or when something we massively hoped for didn't happen. Both elements combined in the mind of Joseph as he finished the task of burying Jesus just before the Sabbath. We all know disappointment and loss at times, and they are hard to take and difficult to think and work through. If we were, in our imagination, to sit next to Joseph on this particular Sabbath, we might hear him talking about Jesus and the hope he had placed in him, we may hear him weeping and there may well be long periods of silence. There was that one Sabbath day's experience of the death of Jesus without the knowledge of his resurrection, and it was hard to take.

We, of course, were not there to meet with the risen Lord, and when we suffer the loss of a loved one there will be no return on the third day. The experience of Joseph and all Jesus' other friends on the Saturday is therefore closer to our own experiences of loss. The advantage we have over them at this point in the story is that we can put our trust in the risen Lord and take comfort in entrusting our loved one into his everlasting arms. This doesn't take away the tears and the pain of loss or suddenly make it alright. But it means that we have a hope that God's love is stronger than death. Joseph has placed Jesus' body in the tomb and rolled an extremely big stone across it. That, it seemed, was that. But Sunday is coming!

Questions: How was Joseph able to show such courage? What difference do you think being a Christian makes at a time of loss?

Prayer: Lord Jesus, as you lay in your tomb, your friends loved you even as they believed they had lost you. Thank you that you did not stay in the tomb! Amen.

Cleopas and his Companion: Luke 24:13-35 'Were not our hearts burning within us' (v 32) (Easter Day)

As a teenager, being a regular supporter of the local football team, the walk home after a defeat, with its disappointment and inevitable discussions with fellow fans about the failings of individual players and the team as a whole, was always a bit of a trudge. It took me a while to realise that the result of any football match is, in the great scheme of things, insignificant.

Two people with far, far more to be disappointed about, are walking back home to Emmaus. They are downcast and it is good that they have each other (they may well have been a married couple). Things have moved on a little since yesterday because of strange reports of an empty tomb and a vision of angels but the penny hasn't yet dropped, and the mood is still one of despondency.

But this is the day that changes everything. As they explain their sadness to the stranger, the continuing problem for Cleopas and his companion, notwithstanding angelic visitations, is the finality of crucifixion – Jesus is dead! It's difficult to know why they failed to recognise him as he walked along, but the intuitive leap required was clearly beyond them. This can happen. I remember some years ago watching a singing competition on television of the kind in which one contestant is knocked out each week until the last two remaining singers battle it out in the final. It wasn't until the very last show that I realised that I had seen one of the finalists performing at a free concert during the Orkney Folk Festival a few years before. At no point during the series up until that point had I made the connection even though I'd been watching her sing every week.

The heart of this beautiful story comes after Cleopas and his companion invite Jesus to stay with them. It is as they are at table that suddenly Jesus, for he it is, takes over the duties of the host. As he takes the bread, gives thanks, breaks it, and begins to give it to them they suddenly see who it is, and we see the unmistakeable shape of the service by which we remember his sacrifice week by week. It is a moment of recognition before Jesus suddenly vanishes. Holy Communion, the Eucharist, Mass, the Lord's Supper, whatever we call it, is not just about remembering events of two thousand years ago, it is about recognising the presence of the living Lord who meets us in bread and wine before sending us out to share the message of God's unconditional love.

As Cleopas and his companion reflect on their experience, they realise that the transformation began on the road when their hearts burned as the 'stranger' opened the Scriptures to them. So it is that on our life journey Jesus is always present even when we don't recognise he's there. We may not feel his presence, we may be too busy to even think about it or we may not be open to the possibility; but he is there. And his risen presence has the power to transform.

The two travellers immediately turn themselves around and head for Jerusalem where they meet the other disciples who are also full of joy having embraced the unlooked-for, unhoped-for truth that Jesus is alive. It seems that by this stage, of the eleven (no Judas, of course), Jesus had as yet appeared only to Peter (given his real name rather than his nickname here – v 34). I would have loved to have been a fly on the wall on that occasion. Not only has Peter had to deal with the death of his great friend and teacher, but he's also had plenty of time to reflect on his own moral failure in denying three times that he had ever had anything to do with him. Jesus has not yet fully restored him and made him ready to lead the church; that comes later in Galilee (John 21:15-17) but nonetheless the joy and the sheer relief of Peter must have been palpable.

It's worth pointing out that this story is about people who initially found the idea that anybody could rise from the dead very difficult to get a handle on; it was every bit as challenging a concept for them as it is in today's secular culture. Cleopas and his companion were intelligent human beings who, as we have seen, were unable to grasp that Jesus was the one walking and talking with them because, to their minds, it simply wasn't possible.

We don't have to throw our brains away to believe that Jesus rose from the dead. It was something he said would happen, there is a solid historical foundation for believing it and it offers us and our distracted generation an entirely new perspective on life. This is not pie in the sky when you die; it is credible truth attested to by many witnesses. We are not just here by chance; we are here because we are children of God. This life is not all there is, it is part of something much greater and more wonderful. In our daily lives we are not left to shift for ourselves, Jesus has promised us his constant presence. The risen Lord offers all of us, along with the repentant criminal, the hope of glory and the assurance that we will be with him for ever.

At each service of Holy Communion, we remember the story of Jesus' suffering and death as we share tokens of bread and wine taking us back to the moment his body was broken and blood poured from the wound in his side. It sounds quite grim put like that. Yet this sacrifice had to be made both to deal with the sins that disfigure our own lives and the world of which we are a part. It was the victory of the risen Lord over sin and death on the cross that opened the way to a sure and certain hope and hands us an invitation to be citizens of the new heaven and new earth (Revelation 21:1). Because Jesus died and rose again, we will see God's kingdom in all its fullness. We dare to hope that it is a kingdom in which there will be no more tears or pain, all wrongs will have been put right and there will be a new heaven and a new earth. If that isn't good news, I don't know what is.

Our call as Christians is to be witnesses to these truths and make them visible in the way we live our lives. We won't be able to do that perfectly because we are all fallible and sometimes make mistakes. Those who saw the risen Jesus after his resurrection were equally fallible, yet many people were blessed and found faith because of their faithful witness. The key thing is that we don't have to live out and share our faith in the risen Lord as if it were all down to us, even though that is too often the way we choose to do it. The Holy Spirit is God's unconditional gift to the whole created order and the one through whom the risen Christ is present with those who believe in him guiding them into all truth (John 16:13), with those working for justice and peace and with all who need to know that they have hope and a future. We can sometimes feel that our day to day lives consist of wandering around on back roads that seem unimportant and insignificant. Yet these old stories intersect profoundly with ours because they assure us that nobody is overlooked, and that God values us all equally for who we are, his deeply beloved children. We are all a small yet infinitely precious part of something that is ineffable; impossible to grasp or fully know and it is in the context of nothing less than the vision of a new heaven and a new earth that we live out our faith and witness to the amazing truth that 'Christ has died, Christ is risen, and Christ will come again'.

Alleluia Christ is risen! He is risen indeed, Alleluia!

Questions: How often do you recognise the presence of Jesus in your life? What might help to make you more aware of it?

Prayer: Risen Lord Jesus, thank you that you are with us today and every moment of our lives. Help us to put our trust in you and to recognise your presence. Amen.